THE
BATTLE
THAT
STOPPED
ROME

THE
BATTLE
THAT
STOPPED
ROME

EMPEROR AUGUSTUS,
ARMINIUS, AND THE
SLAUGHTER OF
THE LEGIONS IN
THE TEUTOBURG FOREST

Peter S. Wells

W · W · NORTON & COMPANY
NEW YORK   LONDON

Frontispiece. Detail of etching by Daniel Nikolaus Chodowiecki showing Arminius surrounded by his people and with fruits of victory, including captured weapons in the foreground and Roman legionary standards in the background. From Anton von Klein, *Leben und Bildnisse der grossen Deutschen,* vol. I (Mannheim, 1782).

Book design by Margaret M. Wagner

Production manager: Julia Druskin

Library of Congress Cataloging-in-Publication Data

Wells, Peter S.

The battle that stopped Rome : Emperor Augustus, Arminius, and the slaughter of the legions in the Teutoburg Forest / Peter S. Wells.—1st ed.

p. cm.

Includes bibliographical references and index.

ISBN 0-393-02028-2 (hardcover)

1. Teutoburger Wald, Battle of, Germany, 9 A.D. 2. Arminius, Prince of the Cherusci.
3. Varus, Publius Quintilius. 4. Augustus, Emperor of Rome, 63 B.C.–14 A.D.
5. Rome—History—Augustus, 30 B.C.–14 A.D. 6. Germany—History—To 843.
7. Romans—Germany—Westphalia. I. Title.

DD123.W45 2003

936.3'02—dc21

2003010789

W. W. Norton & Company, Inc., 500 Fifth Avenue, New York, N.Y. 10110

www.wwnorton.com

W. W. Norton & Company Ltd., Castle House, 75/76 Wells Street, London W1T 3QT

1 2 3 4 5 6 7 8 9 0

To My Family

CONTENTS

APPENDIXES

LIST OF ILLUSTRATIONS

LIST OF MAPS

IMPORTANT DATES

63 B.C.   birth of Octavius, later named Augustus

58–51 B.C.   Julius Caesar campaigns in and conquers Gaul

45 B.C.   Julius Caesar adopts Octavius/Augustus, making him his heir

44 B.C.   Julius Caesar assassinated

27 B.C.   Octavius named Augustus and becomes first Roman emperor

16–13 B.C.   Augustus in Rhineland overseeing buildup of bases

12–9 B.C.   Drusus leads campaigns across Rhine eastward toward Elbe

9–7 B.C.   Tiberius commands Rhine legions, triumph in Rome

A.D. 4-6   Tiberius again commands Rhineland legions

A.D. 7   Varus appointed governor in Rhineland and Germany

A.D. 9   Arminius and the Germans destroy three Roman legions in Battle of the Teutoburg Forest

A.D. *14* Death of Augustus, Tiberius becomes emperor

A.D. *19* Arminius murdered by his fellow Cherusci

1470 Tacitus's *Germania* published in Venice

1505 Tacitus's *Annals* discovered at Corvey, Germany

1875 Statue of Arminius/Hermann completed

1885 Mommsen identifies Kalkriese as site of the battle

1987 Clunn and Schlüter link weapons with battle site

1989 excavations at Kalkriese reveal abundant remains of battle

PREFACE

According to accounts by two great chroniclers of Rome, Tacitus and Cassius Dio, in A.D. 9 a chieftain named Arminius led a massive army of Germanic warriors—"barbarians" to the Romans—in the annihilation of some twenty thousand Roman soldiers. It was one of the most devastating defeats suffered by the Roman army. The effects of this catastrophe were profound. It ended Rome's designs on conquest farther east beyond the Rhine and resulted in the emperor Augustus's decision to expand and strengthen a series of military bases along the Rhine frontier, creating a densely militarized zone in the middle of Europe. As the bases grew, towns were established near them, many of which became major centers of medieval and modern Europe, including Bonn, Cologne, Mainz, and Strasbourg. Furthermore, the Rhine remained the political and cultural boundary of the Roman world throughout the succeeding four centuries of the Roman Empire, and it has continued as a cultural, and often a political, boundary for the past two thousand years. The psychological effect of the crushing defeat on Augustus and his successors contributed to their ending the policy of military expansion not just in Europe but in Africa and Asia as well. This battle truly changed the course of world history.

Though a watershed event, the Battle of the Teutoburg Forest is not well known today. Between the sixteenth century and the mid-twentieth, the story of this great battle was familiar to people in the German-speaking regions of Europe, and the battle became a powerful metaphor for populations struggling to stay free of outside domination. As the hero Arminius, who became known by the German name Hermann during the sixteenth century, decisively defeated the imperialistic Romans, so too sixteenth-century humanists, including Martin Luther, struggled to be free of the dictates of the Roman Church. In the nineteenth century, the heroic tradition of Arminius was invoked to confront another threatening foreign power—the France of Napoleon and his successors. After the First World War, and with the profound political and ideological changes of the twentieth century, the popularity of the Arminius/Hermann story waned. Yet, for historians trying to understand Roman policy in northern Europe, the event remains critically important.

Until very recently, all of the information about the great battle consisted of several brief descriptions in texts by Roman and Greek writers that were preserved in European monasteries and church collections through the Middle Ages, and a single inscribed gravestone commemorating a centurion who fell in the conflict. None of the descriptions were eyewitness accounts, and most were written generations and even centuries after the event. The accounts are contradictory. Yet, the historical descriptions of the reactions of the emperor Augustus to this military disaster make clear how important it was.

Everything has changed now in terms of our ability to understand the battle. After many centuries of searching, the actual site of the battle was discovered in 1987, and archaeological excavations carried out every year since then are yielding details about exactly where and how the battle happened. We now have access to information about the course of the battle, about the tactics used by both sides, and about the immediate outcome. As the archaeological investigations progress, this battle is becoming one of the best-documented confrontations from ancient times. Instead of relying on accounts written by witnesses—of which there were none in A.D. 9—who can transmit only what they as individuals saw, heard from others, or thought, the archaeological evidence permits us to examine the physical remains of the battle directly.

The Battle of the Teutoburg Forest was fundamentally different from another battle involving Roman legions that has become familiar to tens of millions of filmgoers. The re-created battle that opens the hugely successful movie *Gladiator* was based on an event almost two hundred years after the confrontation that forms the focus of this book. That later battle was also fought against Germanic peoples of central Europe, but it took place on the Danube frontier near the modern city of Vienna, about four hundred miles southeast of Kalkriese, the site of our battle. The Roman uniforms and weapons shown in the film are similar to what the earlier legionaries had with them in the Teutoburg Forest, though styles and equipment changed slightly during the intervening years. The fundamental difference is that in the battle depicted in the film the Roman commander chose the site for battle and planned the assault, and the legions were able to assemble their artillery and launch their attack from an open field, according to well-established and carefully planned procedures. In the Teutoburg Forest, their enemy chose the location—Arminius and his Germanic warriors launched a surprise attack on the Roman soldiers—and the ambush on the marching column of troops took place in a forested and marshy landscape where the legions could offer little effective defense.

The results of the ongoing excavations at Kalkriese enable us to understand in ever-increasing detail what happened in that epic confrontation. At least as important is the accumulating information about the late Iron Age Germanic peoples of northern continental Europe that allows us to understand something that the Romans never could—how these tribal communities, whom the Romans dismissed as primitive, nomadic barbarians, were able to catch the Roman commanders completely off guard and wipe out three entire legions of the most powerful army in the world.

Augustus and his fellow Romans never grasped how this could have happened. As we will see, they completely misjudged the peoples of the forests of northern Europe, their way of life, their technology, and their political systems. This fundamental lack of understanding led to Rome's great military loss and to the permanent cultural frontier at the Rhine.

The epic battles that have shaped European history, from Hastings to Waterloo and the Allied landings on D-day, have been thoroughly studied for generations. At long last, the full story of perhaps the most important battle in European history can be told, and that is what I shall do in the pages that follow.

My narrative is based on the surviving Roman texts, the archaeology of the battle site, and the results of investigations by archaeologists of hundreds of Iron Age and Roman period settlements and cemeteries in northern central Europe. My account is written for a modern audience, and I treat cause and effect in ways that I believe will make sense to such a readership. As we learn from accounts written by Roman historians two thousand years ago, Roman observers often explained events in terms of religious rituals properly or improperly conducted, of omens, such as flights of birds or halos around the sun, and of the personal failings of individuals. An explanation for the outcome of the Battle of the Teutoburg Forest that might have made sense to a Roman in A.D. 9 might not satisfy an American reader in 2003, and vice versa.

Professional archaeologists and historians, with their awareness of the complexity, ambiguity, and incompleteness of evidence regarding the distant human past, are typically very cautious in their interpretations, carefully supporting all of their assertions with reference to specific evidence. But in order to make the subjects they research interesting and worthwhile to the general public, they must sometimes depart from their scholarly procedures and take chances in making informed guesses to fill gaps in the hard evidence. Parts of this book, primarily in chapters 1, 8, 9, and 10, are carefully crafted historical speculations. By this I mean that I have taken the known facts and woven a narrative that is plausible and consistent with those facts. Although archaeology and history provide us with the general outlines of the event and its background, and great detail about some specific matters, much is unknown. In order to create a coherent story, I need to fill in those details, using my judgment as to how things might have happened. In the bibliographical essay at the end of the book, I make clear which parts of the presentation are based on solid evidence and which parts are reconstructions.

There are two important reasons for taking the initiative to develop a coherent narrative. One is to create a story. Neither archaeological evidence nor ancient texts are self-explanatory. Both kinds of information need to be integrated into a narrative in order for them to make sense. In scholarly contexts, that narrative is usually based on specific theoretical concerns of the day. My aim here is to make this story accessible to general readers who are not necessarily interested in current theoretical debates in anthropology, archaeology, or history. This account is therefore not burdened with theoretical frameworks from those disciplines, but attempts to provide a coherent narrative that will be readily understandable to the general reader. I hope through this approach to show the reader unfamiliar with archaeology how valuable a source of information it can be for understanding the past.

Furthermore, in considering an event such as this great battle, we must think about the impact of the experience on the people who were part of it. Historical and archaeological treatments of even such dramatic and emotional events as battles are usually coolly analytical, striving to be objective. But combat is not objective for the participants—it is a highly emotional, terrifying experience that no participant ever forgets. In chapters 1, 8, and 9, I try at least to suggest what the scene might have been like for the Roman soldiers and the Germanic warriors who fought in the battle in September of A.D. 9.

The second major reason for my using this approach is to challenge professional archaeologists and historians involved in the study of the battle and its background. Most of us who work in the fields of anthropology, archaeology, and history focus our research and writing efforts on specific data and research questions. In this time of great specialization in the academic world, it is difficult for any professional scholar to develop the "big picture," and most shy away from the attempt. Unfortunately, as a result, we sometimes lose sight of important issues. The interested public often remains uninformed about new research, and professional scholars sometimes neglect to place their work into a context that will be of use and interest to others. By developing this "big picture" through the use of historical speculation, I hope to stimulate my colleagues to pose some of the larger questions about the meanings behind their data.

Throughout the text, I refer to the two sides in the conflict as Romans and Germans. At the outset, I need to clarify these terms. The soldiers who served under the Roman commander Varus were either members of the Roman Seventeenth, Eighteenth, and Nineteenth Legions, or they were auxiliary troops employed by the Roman army. Some of the men came from Italy (we know that Marcus Caelius, whose gravestone survives, was from Bologna), but many were probably from other parts of the Empire, such as Gaul (modern France, Belgium, and Germany and the Netherlands west and south of the Rhine River), and perhaps even from as far away as North Africa and Syria. Some of the auxiliaries may have been members of tribal groups from the unconquered lands east of the Rhine. Thus, when I refer to these soldiers as Romans, it is only in the sense that they were in the service of the Roman Empire. Individually, many may have thought of themselves as being something other than Roman.

By the time of the events discussed in this book, Roman authorities considered all of the peoples who lived in the lands east of the Rhine in the central part of continental Europe to be Germans. The earliest detailed description of these peoples is in the writings of Julius Caesar from around 50 B.C. Roman military commanders were not overly concerned with the ways that indigenous peoples identified themselves, and it is certain that the Roman use of the term "German" to name all of the peoples east of the Rhine was a lumping together of diverse groups throughout a large region. Until the Roman army began to threaten them, first with Caesar's incursions in 55 and 53 B.C. and later with the campaigns of Drusus and Tiberius that began in 12 B.C., the myriad peoples whom the Romans called Germans probably did not even think of themselves as a single group (just as the peoples of the Americas did not consider themselves all part of one entity, though Columbus called them all Indians).

Thus, the names "Roman" and "German" are both complex terms. But as I use them in this text, they refer simply to members of the two opposing military forces that clashed in A.D. 9.

THE
BATTLE
THAT
STOPPED
ROME

1

AMBUSHED!

The early afternoon sun reflected off the gleaming armor of
Publius Quinctilius Varus as he rode along the track at the base
of the hills that formed the southern edge of the North
European Plain. His personal bodyguards surrounded him. At
the front and rear of the long column marched auxiliary and
cavalry units. Varus and his entourage were in the midst of the
thousands of troops that made up his three legions. From his
horse, Varus could see only a small portion of the immense column of soldiers as it moved along the track through woods and
glades. This was new territory into which he and his legions
now ventured, north of the routes that the Roman forces were
accustomed to taking on their way to and from summer campaigns in the Germanic wilderness east of the Rhine River.

On this September day in A.D. 9, Varus commanded an army
of some eighteen thousand troops. It consisted of the
Seventeenth, Eighteenth, and Nineteenth Legions—the crack
professional infantry of the Roman army—together with auxiliary forces of three cavalry units and six more cohorts of
infantry. This fighting force presented a colorful picture of men,
horses, and wagons, as it marched steadily along the beaten, but
narrow, path through the northern European wilderness. Each of
Varus's three legions proudly displayed its traditions on the tall
staff that bore the legion's name and number, along with an
image of the imperial Roman eagle—the symbol for which the

soldiers were willing to fight and die. The shiny helmets, glinting armor, brightly colored uniforms, silver and gold decorations on the garments and weapons of the officers, and richly ornamented harnesses of the cavalry horses created an extraordinary spectacle as the army marched relentlessly forward. The clanking of armor, the pounding of the soldiers' hobnailed boots, and the creaking of the supply wagons produced a cacophony foreign to this sparsely populated region.

They were marching to finish the conquering of a province, just as Julius Caesar had done two generations earlier in Gaul. The catalyst for this march was information provided by a local chieftain known as Arminius, whom Varus trusted and believed to be a strong supporter of the Roman cause. Arminius had served with the Roman military as a commander of an auxiliary unit and had distinguished himself on the field of battle. Days earlier, he had told the Roman commander of an uprising started by a small tribe that lived a day or two's march west of the Roman camp near the Weser River. Segestes, like Arminius a member of the Cherusci tribe, had warned Varus of possible treachery by Arminius, but Varus had grown to trust Arminius and his comrades and discounted Segestes' concerns. The day before, Varus had set out from the Roman camp with his army, heading toward the reported uprising. This was the same direction in which Varus was planning to march anyway, back to his winter base at Xanten (Vetera) on the Rhine, and attending to the small revolt would require only a small detour. Varus departed with the understanding that Arminius would go ahead to rally some of his own tribesmen to join in the quashing of the rebellion. Since Varus expected to encounter no dangers in this now largely pacified region until he reached the territory of the rebellious group, he took no unusual precautions in the marching order of his troops.

The route took the Roman army westward from its summer base near the Weser, along the northern edge of the hills known as the Wiehengebirge. This range of west–east-running hills forms the boundary between the flat sandy landscape of the North European Plain and the hilly countryside of the central European uplands. The Roman troop train marched along the flat terrain on the very southern edge of the North European Plain, with the Wiehengebirge to its left. Varus and his officers were unfamiliar with this route, because all of the Roman campaigning in Germany over the past twenty years had been to the south in the hilly upland territories. In those regions, the passing of earlier units on summer campaigns had resulted in the clearing of substantial tracks through the forests, and in the bridging of numerous streams, so movement of troops was now relatively easy. But the stretches where Varus and his army marched this day had seen no such improvements by the military engineers, and the going was rough. The track they followed was well worn by the local peoples, but in many places the legions had difficulty marching six abreast, as was their custom in such landscapes where the passage was narrow. Often troops in the vanguard had to clear fallen trees from the path and fill deep muddy holes in order to let the wagons pass.

Much of the land through which they marched was covered by woods, mainly mixed oak forest with birch, beech, and alder trees. In some places, the forest was dense and gloomy and the path even narrower than usual. In others, the trees had been cleared away for farmland and meadow, and the Romans felt a sense of relief each time they emerged from the dark forest into the clearings. In the open areas, the track edge was lined with high yellow grasses and late summer wildflowers. The soldiers passed fields of wheat and barley, meadows in which cows had recently grazed, and sturdy farmhouses. Yet they saw hardly a soul along their route. The locals, alarmed at the menacing sounds of the approaching troops, had fled with their cattle into the woods long before any Romans could catch sight of them. Bogs, marshes, and ponds were common in this low-lying region at the base of the hills, and the passing troops often had to skirt these impediments.

When they approached the Kalkrieser Berg, a 350-foot-high hill that juts out northward from the range, the troops had to turn north for about two miles to go around it. This route took them into an hourglass-shaped passage barely half a mile wide in the middle and four miles long, just north of the steep hill and along the southern edge of a huge bog (see maps 3, 8, and 9). Even under the best of circumstances, this passage was treacherous. Numerous wide, muddy streams meandered across it, flowing north from the hills into the Great Bog. Pools and swampy areas impeded progress, and in places the forest was so dense that the marching formation had to split as soldiers moved around trees and cautiously avoided exposed roots. Within this passage, most of the ground was saturated with water from the bog and the streams flowing toward it. Only a strip of sandy ground about one hundred yards wide located at the southern edge of the passage, close to the base of the hill, offered somewhat more solid footing. The troops marched along this narrow isthmus through the passage, with the forested slopes close on their left and stands of willows and alders amid the reeds and sedges bordering the Great Bog on their right. Where streams cut through the narrow walkway, managing the supply wagons became particularly difficult. This was not a place in which a Roman commander felt comfortable. But turning around a two-mile-long marching column of troops to seek an alternative route was out of the question at this stage.

Suddenly a chilling yell was heard as attackers on all sides fell upon the struggling Romans. Varus and his army were caught completely off guard and in the worst possible situation. They had not been marching in a formation that permitted rapid transition into fighting mode, nor were they accustomed to combat in forested and marshy environments. They had been lured into a perfect trap. The attackers darted from behind trees, hurling their spears at their victims. Stuck among the trees and ankle-deep in slippery mud, the Roman soldiers had neither room to maneuver nor the possibility of escape. Hundreds of men were impaled by the attackers' iron-tipped spears. Some died instantly; others screamed in agony as they tried desperately to pull the spears from their bodies. When they realized that the Roman soldiers were unable to mount any effective defense, the attackers left the shelter of the surrounding trees and moved in with their swords, stabbing and slashing wildly, cutting down hundreds more victims. The Roman troops were thrown into chaos, as thousands lay dead or dying of their wounds on the muddy and now blood-soaked earth.

The native warriors were not as heavily armed as the Roman legionaries—they had few helmets or sets of body armor—and depended instead upon the effectiveness of their spears and long swords. In the open field, the heavily armed and highly disciplined Roman troops would have prevailed, even if outnumbered by the native forces. But the surprise attack in this confined and marshy environment put the Roman troops at a severe disadvantage. The natives knew the terrain, and their weapons and fighting tactics were much better suited to it than were those of the Romans.

Varus and his commanders quickly realized that they had been lured into a deadly trap. In his fear and desperation verging on panic, Varus felt the full force of Arminius's duplicity.

2

CREATION OF THE LEGEND

Arminius and German National Identity

The Battle of the Teutoburg Forest was virtually forgotten during the Middle Ages, when traditions of recording history and of reading and writing declined. Some vague memories of it probably survived in songs and legends, such as the stories of Siegfried the Dragon Slayer, most familiar today in the form of Wagner's Ring Cycle of operas. Though little known during the Middle Ages outside of religious establishments, many ancient texts were preserved, and copied when manuscripts deteriorated, in monasteries and churches. It was not until the Renaissance, about 1300–1550, when manuscripts of the ancient Greek and Roman writers were sought out, rediscovered, read, translated, and circulated, that the story of the Battle of the Teutoburg Forest became familiar again.

Interest in the ancient inhabitants of northern Europe, whom the Romans called Germans, and in Arminius in particular, became especially intense following the discovery, during the fifteenth and early sixteenth centuries, of two texts written by the Roman historian Tacitus. By 1425, news had spread among scholars, particularly in Italy, that monasteries in Germany and neighboring regions north of the Alps preserved important manuscripts of Roman authors. Poggio Bracciolini (1380–1459), a prime mover among the Italian humanists, contacted a monk at the monastery of Hersfeld, in central Germany, about gaining

access to manuscripts by Tacitus (see map 1). He visited manuscript collections in monasteries and churches at Cologne, Fulda,
Hersfeld, and Reichenau in Germany and at St. Gall in
Switzerland. It is not clear to what extent he copied manuscripts,
or arranged to have them copied, and to what extent he acquired
them. In his letters, Bracciolini wrote that he intended to "liber-
ate manuscripts from the dungeons of the barbarians"—his way
of saying that he wanted to get them out of the monastic libraries
of northern Europe and into the hands of the humanists working in Italy. This sentiment suggests that he acquired some
original manuscripts. At least one modern scholar has compared
this activity to the more recent acquisition by European muse-

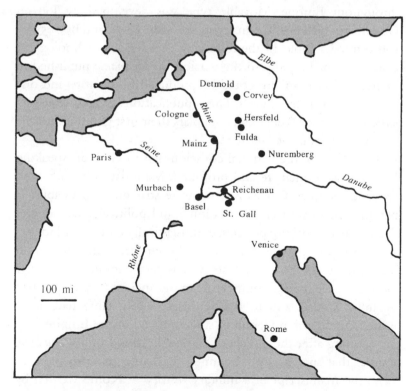

Map 1. Map showing places mentioned in chapter 2.

ums of art treasures from the ancient civilizations of Egypt, Greece, and Mesopotamia.

The most important description of the peoples whom the Romans called Germans is in Tacitus's work known as the *Germania*, written around A.D. 100 and found by Bracciolini at Hersfeld In 1431, a colleague of Bracciolini's, Niccolò Niccoli, created a handwritten copy of it. Either the original or a copy was brought to Rome, perhaps by Bracciolini, perhaps by an associate, sometime in the 1450s. There a number of scholars copied the *Germania* by hand. It was first published in 1470 in Venice and in Germany in 1473, in Nuremberg.

The reason why this work could have such a large impact is that at just this time the printing press was being adopted in cities throughout Europe. Movable type was developed by Johann Gutenberg in Mainz, Germany, in the early 1450s, and by 1455 he had printed a Bible. In the following decades, the technology of printing spread rapidly, so the versions of *Germania* published in Venice and Nuremberg could be produced in quantity and disseminated to many readers. These publications offered relatively large numbers of Renaissance scholars their first glimpse into the world of the ancient Germans.

The effect on the national consciousness of German-speaking Europe was immediate and profound. Many late fifteenth- and sixteenth-century Germans, who were struggling to establish a national identity to create a cultural and political unity among the German-speaking peoples, enthusiastically embraced Tacitus's descriptions of peoples they deemed their direct ancestors from the time when Europe's history was just beginning. Tacitus's Germans gave them a counterpart to the ancient Gauls described by Julius Caesar and to the Romans whose fame had never waned during the millennium since the end of the Empire.

Not long after the discovery and publication of the *Germania*, sources that specifically mentioned the battle came to light. In 1470, the manuscript of a military history of Rome written by

Lucius Annaeus Florus was found in Paris. It contained a description of the defeat of the Roman general Quinctilius Varus at the hands of the Germans. An account of the discovery, by the Roman general Germanicus, of the site of the battle six years after it was fought, contained in the *Annals* of Tacitus, was discovered in 1505 in a ninth-century copy preserved at the monastery at Corvey, in central Germany. That manuscript was brought to Rome about 1508 and published there in 1515. This account by Tacitus is the only one that provides a description of the location of the battle, near the headwaters of the Ems and Lippe Rivers, in northwestern Germany, near what Tacitus calls the *saltus Teutoburgiensis*, the Teutoburg Forest. Tacitus is thus a central figure, both in contributing important details about the story of Arminius and in providing us with our only ethnography of the ancient Germans.

The same year that Tacitus's *Annals* were published, 1515, the German humanist Benatus Rhenanus located, at the Benedictine abbey at Murbach, in Alsace, a manuscript of the *Roman History* by Velleius Paterculus. Unlike Tacitus and Florus, that author was a contemporary of the battle, and he probably even knew personally both the victor, Arminius, and the defeated Roman governor, Varus. This manuscript was published in Rome in 1515 and in Basel, Switzerland, in 1520. In it, the author provides the critical details about the number of Roman units that were annihilated in the battle—three legions, three cavalry units, and six infantry cohorts. Velleius describes Arminius and his cunning plans and lays the blame for the catastrophe on the incompetence of the Roman commander, Varus.

The humanists' discovery and publication of these manuscripts had important literary and political effects. Arminius became a favorite literary subject. In the 1520s, Ulrich von Hutten composed a drama about Arminius in which the Germanic hero argues, in the warrior's heaven Elysium, that he deserves to be considered history's greatest general, grander even than

Alexander the Great and Hannibal. In the context of political and religious struggles of the time, Hutten and other writers seized especially upon Tacitus's description of Arminius as the "liberator of Germany" to create a hero of national proportions.

Martin Luther was enmeshed in his own struggles with Rome, both over theological doctrine and over what he considered the right of Germans to manage their own church affairs independently of the powers in Rome. In his writings, he expressed admiration for Arminius and his deeds, crediting him as the savior and liberator of his people. Luther may have been the first writer to Germanicize the Latin name Arminius into "Hermann," the name by which the increasingly mythologized hero was known to later generations of nationalistic enthusiasts. The ruling elites of German-speaking Europe eagerly adopted the elaborate mythology that developed around the idea of Arminius/Hermann. He emerged as the guarantor of German freedom against the outside aggressor, and his heroic victory over the Roman army was viewed as a great unifying theme for what was, until 1871, a culture divided into a large number of small political entities, unlike the centralized kingdoms of England and France.

Numerous woodcuts, engravings, and paintings representing Arminius and the battle provided visual imagery to associate with the developing legend (see illustrations 1–2). The first known picture of the battle is a woodcut produced in 1517 for the title page of Benatus Rhenanus's edition of Velleius Paterculus's *Roman History*, published in 1520. Between 1676 and 1910, no fewer than seventy-six operas about Hermann were written and performed. By the late eighteenth century, the Hermann theme had achieved immense national popularity, and Heinrich Kleist's play *Die Herrmannsschlacht* (Hermann's Battle), first performed in 1860, became widely staged and extremely popular at a time when the nations of Europe were struggling to define their national identities. The German public easily saw a connection between the ancient hero Hermann and the current chancellor Otto von Bismarck, the unifier of Germany in 1871.

Two months after the establishment of the German Empire in that year, the distinguished Roman historian Theodor Mommsen made an explicit connection between Arminius's fight for freedom against Roman domination and the unification of Germany in his own time. In a lecture presented that year about Augustus's policy in Germany, Mommsen referred to the Battle of the Teutoburg Forest as a turning point in world history.

The clearest sign of nineteenth-century enthusiasm for Arminius/Hermann as national hero was the erection of an enormous statue of him high on a hilltop in what is today called the Teutoburg Forest near the small city of Detmold, in northern Germany (see illustration 3). The name Teutoburger Wald (Teutoburg Forest) was adopted in the seventeenth century from Tacitus's term *saltus Teutoburgiensis*, which he located only vaguely, and given to the hilly landscape that now bears that name. As the new archaeological discoveries demonstrate, it is twenty miles south of where the great battle took place. The foundation stone was set in 1841, and the statue was finally dedicated in 1875, just four years after the unification of Germany. The copper figure of Hermann is 87 feet tall (the sword he holds aloft is 23 feet long), standing on a stone base 88 feet high, all atop the Grotenburg hill, 1,300 feet above the surrounding plain. (The Statue of Liberty in New York harbor, also made of copper, was erected in 1886 and stands 152 feet high on a 150-foot pedestal. The Statue of Liberty is thus bigger, but it is not situated on top of a 1,300-foot-high hill.) Hermann's raised sword points westward, toward France, another outside power that had threatened German independence several times in the preceding century. Inscriptions in niches in the monument base commemorate wars of liberation fought against Napoleon in the years 1813–15 and subsequent conflicts with France in 1870 and 1871. Today the monument is described as the most popular tourist site in Germany, with between one and two million visitors each year.

In the fervently nationalistic nineteenth century, the legend of Hermann the liberator and embodiment of German identity reached beyond the borders of Germany and the shores of Europe. When in 1840 a group of New Yorkers of German ancestry founded a nationwide organization to help preserve their language and traditions, they named it the Sons of Herman. The organization grew rapidly during the latter part of the nineteenth century. Members in southwest Minnesota sponsored a half-size replica of the Hermann statue, completed in 1897, which still stands, sword raised on high, overlooking the town of New Ulm. Like many German-oriented cultural entities in the United States, the Sons of Herman declined in popularity during and after World War I. Yet, the organization still survives in many local configurations. For example, the Order of the Sons of Hermann in the State of Texas boasts 78,000 members today.

In Germany at the start of the twentieth century, "Hermann, the liberator of Germany," was a part of the historical instruction in the elementary school curriculum, an indication of how familiar to all the story was at the time. Historians mark the end of the greatest enthusiasm for Hermann at 1918, with the end of the First World War and of the German Empire. But under the Nazi regime, with the official emphasis on the special character of German prehistory and early history, the importance of Hermann's liberating of Germany again came to the fore.

After the Second World War, as school plans were developed anew in the 1950s and 1960s, emphasis in the teaching of early German history was placed on the cooperation between Romans and Germans, not on their conflicts. In a new curriculum introduced in the state of Baden-Württemberg in 1979, for example, the old theme of "Arminius and Varus" was lacking entirely, a profound change from the past.

3

HISTORY AND ARCHAEOLOGY
OF THE BATTLE

We have two completely different sources of information about the battle. One consists of accounts written by Roman and Greek historians, none of them eyewitnesses to the event. The other is the archaeological evidence, most of it recovered and analyzed since 1987.

The Roman Accounts

The earliest known mention of the battle is in a passage of the Roman poet Ovid's "Sorrows" written in the spring of A.D. 10, just a few months after the disaster. In another passage in the same work, this one composed in A.D. 11, Ovid writes, in reference to Arminius, "this traitor . . . trapped our men in a treacherous place—the one who now conceals his unkempt face with his long hair. [With him] . . . was the priest who sacrificed captives to a god who often refused them." Around this same time in his poem "Astronomica," Marcus Manilius also writes of the battle. As an example of "sudden insurrection, and arms uplifted in stealthy treachery," he writes "in foreign parts, when, its oaths forsworn, barbarous Germany made away with our commander Varus and stained the fields with three legions' blood." The emphasis in these writings on what the authors felt was treachery on the part of the Germans is ironic, since the

Germans were trying to protect themselves against Roman conquest.

In A.D. 18 or slightly earlier, the Greek geographer Strabo similarly represents the disaster as an example of untrustworthiness on the part of the Germans. "Those who have been trusted have done the greatest harm, as, for instance, the Cherusci and their subjects, in whose country three Roman legions, with their general Quinctilius Varus, were destroyed by ambush in violation of the treaty."

Three Roman authors, and one Greek writer (Cassius Dio), provide more detail. Each differs from the others in significant ways. The order in which I present them here is based on the kinds of information about the battle that is provided in each account.

VELLEIUS PATERCULUS

The earliest is in the *Roman History* written by Velleius Paterculus, a work published in Rome in A.D. 30. Velleius had been a military officer, and he is likely to have known both Arminius and Varus personally through common service in the Roman army. Velleius provides the information that Arminius had served with the Roman army, been made a Roman citizen, and been granted equestrian rank. His account includes the numerical details about three legions, three cavalry units, and six auxiliary cohorts lost in the battle; it notes that news of the disaster reached Rome just five days after the end of the war in Pannonia and Dalmatia (see below). The account of the battle is abbreviated; Velleius states that he plans to describe the battle in greater detail in another work, but that work does not survive, if he ever wrote it.

Velleius places blame for the disaster on the negligence of Varus, the treachery of Arminius, and the highly disadvantageous environment of forests and swamps in which the Romans were ambushed. His colorful portrayal of the event comes through well even in translation:

An army unexcelled in bravery, the first of Roman armies in discipline, in energy, and in experience in the field, through the negligence of its general, the perfidy of the enemy, and the unkindness of fortune was surrounded. . . . Hemmed in by forests and ambuscades, it was exterminated almost to a man by the very enemy whom it has always slaughtered like cattle. . . .

Velleius tells of Varus's suicide when the battle appeared lost, the beheading of Varus's corpse, the delivering of the head to Maroboduus, the leader of a group of Germanic tribes to the east and southeast, and his sending it on to Augustus in Rome, where it was honorably buried in the family mausoleum. He also recounts the desertion of Vala Numonius, an officer in Varus's army, and his cavalry troops, who fled toward the Rhine, only to be captured and killed by the enemy.

CASSIUS DIO

Cassius Dio, writing a history of Rome at the beginning of the third century, provides a description of the circumstances leading up to the battle and the most detailed account of the battle itself. According to him, at this time Rome controlled parts, but not all, of the regions east of the Rhine. In the areas under their control, Roman troops remained year-round, and the Romans were establishing cities. The local peoples were becoming gradually accustomed to Roman institutions. But as governor, Varus was moving too fast in introducing Roman customs and imposing new regulations. He treated the local people like slaves and demanded exorbitant taxes.

As a result, leaders of the indigenous peoples developed a plan to rid themselves of Varus and his administration. Arminius and his father, Segimer, co-conspirators in the plan to lure Varus and his legions into their trap, gained Varus's unwavering confidence, even joining him regularly at his dinner table. Dio's account includes details about Segestes—leader of a rival faction among the Cherusci who favored cooperation with Rome—warning Varus about the conspiracy, and Varus's refusal to listen. He portrays Varus as an easily fooled individual. When the conspirators inform him that an uprising by a group some distance away requires his attention, the commander leads his troops in that direction, directly into the waiting ambush.

Dio provides the most dramatic account of the battle itself. He describes hilly terrain in which the Romans were attacked, large trees that the troops had to fell in order to let the baggage wagons pass, and a long marching column that included women and children along with troops and supplies. His account includes a severe wind and rain storm, falling tree limbs, wet and treacherous terrain underfoot, and, at the worst possible moment, the surprise attack.

> The mountains had an uneven surface broken by ravines, and the trees grew close together and very high. Hence the Romans, even before the enemy assailed them, were having a hard time of it felling trees, building roads, and bridging places that required it. They had with them many waggons and many beasts of burden as in time of peace; moreover, not a few women and children and a large retinue of servants. . . . Meanwhile a violent rain and wind came up that separated them still further, while the ground, that had become slippery around the roots and logs, made walking very treacherous for them, and the tops of the trees kept breaking off and falling down, causing much confusion. While the Romans were in such difficulties, the barbarians suddenly surrounded them on all sides at once. . . . At first they hurled their volleys from a distance; then, as no one defended himself and many were wounded, they approached closer to them.

Dio's account describes three days of attacks and utterly inadequate Roman defense. Hemmed in by trees and drenched by constant rain, the legionaries are unable to use their weapons effectively. The first night, the Roman troops hastily build a camp, and later destroy all of the wagons and baggage they do not need, to keep supplies from falling into the enemy's hands. The second day, they continue the march, only to be attacked again when they reenter wooded land. The third day, the Romans are surrounded. Varus and other officers, seeing that their situation is hopeless, fall on their swords, and the other Romans die in a bloodbath.

This author goes on to provide important information about Augustus's response to the news of the disaster. According to Dio, Augustus feared that Arminius would attack the Roman bases on the Rhine and perhaps invade Gaul and even Italy. As a result of violent migrations during earlier times in the city's history (see chapter 7), Romans had real fears of invasion by barbarians from the north. Augustus dismissed the Gauls and Germans in his personal bodyguard and sent others residing in Rome away, fearing that they might incite an uprising.

After it became clear that no further disasters would ensue immediately, Augustus pondered probable causes of the catastrophe. He recalled various portents that suggested that Varus's defeat had been caused by an angry god. Lightning had struck a temple of Mars, a swarm of locusts was seen in Rome, Alpine peaks were observed to emit fire, numerous comets appeared in the sky, and a statue of Victory in the Rhineland turned, from facing east toward the unconquered tribes, to facing toward the south and Italy. Augustus and his advisers tried to interpret this disaster in terms of their understanding of the major forces in world events. According to this passage in Dio's text, something as unexpected as the catastrophe in the northern forests could be explained only in terms of profound dislocation in the natural, human, and spiritual worlds.

LUCIUS ANNAEUS FLORUS

In his brief account of the battle in his history of Rome, written around the middle of the second century A.D., Florus states many of the essential points made by Velleius Paterculus and other authors. He mentions the Germans' resistance to the policies introduced by Varus, Segestes' warnings to Varus of a plot against him, and Varus's refusal to heed those warnings. In contrast to Cassius Dio's detailed account of the continuous assaults during the Roman march, Florus's describes a massive attack on Varus's troops in their temporary base camp, where Varus as governor had begun the process of administering justice in this soon-to-be province. The Germans overrun the camp, annihilate the three legions, and seize all of the materials remaining in the camp as their booty. Florus conveys a horrific image of barbarian outrages:

> Never was slaughter more cruel than took place there in the marshes and woods, never were more intolerable insults inflicted by barbarians. . . . They put out the eyes of some of them and cut off the hands of others. . . .

According to Florus, at the time he was writing, in the mid-second century, two of the eagles that had been captured in the battle remained in the possession of the German tribes. In the heat of the battle, the standard-bearer removed the third eagle from its staff and hid it in the marsh to keep it from falling into the enemy's hands.

P. CORNELIUS TACITUS

Tacitus, considered by many to be Rome's greatest historian, informs us in his *Annals* about the aftermath of the battle. He wrote his account in the early years of the second century, on the basis of research in archives in Rome. According to Tacitus, during Roman campaigns in A.D. 15 (see chapter 11), six years after the battle, the general Stertinius recovers the eagle of the Nineteenth Legion from among equipment abandoned by the Bructeri after a battle with Roman troops. Tacitus then describes the visit by the commander Germanicus and the consul Caecina to the site of the great battle of A.D. 9. They come upon what Tacitus calls Varus's first camp, "with its broad sweep and measured spaces for officer and eagles." It is uncertain whether Tacitus means a base camp at which Varus and his troops spent part of the summer, or the camp hurriedly erected the first night after the attack. Next he describes "a half-ruined wall and shallow ditch . . . [where] . . . the now broken remnant had taken cover." The spatial relationship between the two camps is unclear in Tacitus's text—was the second inside the first, or some distance away?

Germanicus and his men see the whitened bones of fallen soldiers on the ground, skulls still nailed to trees, and bones of horses. Nearby are "savage altars" where the victorious Germans killed the officers they had captured. In this account, soldiers who survived the battle and returned with Germanicus point out the spots where Varus was wounded and where he fell on his sword, where legionary eagles were seized, and where the victors slaughtered their Roman prisoners.

The Archaeology

The modern visitor to Kalkriese would have no reason to think that a seminal event in world history had happened there. There is no immense river to form a frontier between peoples, such as the Rhine or the Danube (see maps 2 and 3). There are no high mountains or deep valleys to present obstacles, or easy opportunities, for the marches of conquering armies. Nor are there vast expanses of fertile soil that might yield precious surpluses of grain.

When you leave the town of Bramsche heading east on the two-lane highway, on your right rise the Wiehengebirge, while on your left the land slopes down toward the north. The eleva-

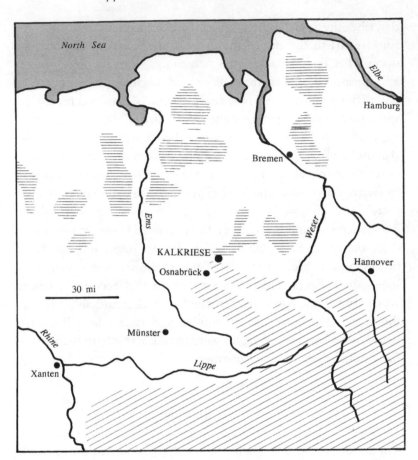

Map 2. Topographical map showing Kalkriese, site of the battle, in its geographical situation in northern Germany. Major rivers and modern cities are indicated. Oblique hatching: hilly uplands. Horizontal hatching: regions of bog land.

tion of the road changes little as it wends toward the south about seven miles east of Bramsche, but here the slope on the south side of the road becomes steeper. The base of this hill, the Kalkrieser Berg, is cultivated; only slightly higher up, however, the land is forested. At this point, the road seems to cling to the base of the slope as it rounds the hill toward the village of Venne.

On a typical summer morning, farmers drive their tractors between the fields, truck drivers roar along the small highway, and local residents go about their daily business in the villages or in Bramsche. Home owners work in their yards, and in the village of Kalkriese mechanics repair cars at an auto shop. On a recent visit, I was struck by the dissonance between the images of the great battle I was there to study and the apparently serene and comfortable lives of the modern inhabitants. Of course, A.D. 9 was far from the last time that people of central Europe experienced mass bloodshed and destruction. But the confrontation that happened in this quiet landscape was unique in Europe's history.

Discovery of the Battle Site

During the past several centuries, many investigators tried to identify the place in northern Germany where the great battle had occurred. Hundreds of books and articles—popular and scholarly—argued the merits of one location over others in this quest for the battle site. The historical information about the event preserved in the texts by Roman writers is so scanty and vague that many different places in northern Germany seemed potential candidates. But early on in the search, there was reason to suspect Kalkriese as the location. Already in a publication of 1716, Zacharias Goeze, a local theologian and philosopher with an interest in numismatics, mentioned Roman coins found by farmers at Kalkriese. The earliest detailed report about such finds dates to 1768, when the scholar and governmental official Justus Möser observed that in the course of digging turf, composting organic materials, and cultivating the soil, farmers often came across coins. In 1885, in a study titled *Die Örtlichkeit der Varusschlacht* (The Location of the Varus Battle), the historian Theodor Mommsen proposed, on the basis of the accumulating coin finds, this very location as the site. But so many Roman coins are found throughout northern Germany that Mommsen's suggested linking of this spot with the great conflict lacked convincing supporting evidence.

In July of 1987, Tony Clunn, an officer in the British army stationed at Osnabrück, in northwestern Germany, discovered the ancient battle site that had eluded archaeologists and historians who had been searching for it for over six centuries. Clunn had an avocational interest in history and in ancient coins. After arriving in Osnabrück, he went to see the head of archaeology in the region, Dr. Wolfgang Schlüter, to inquire whether he might explore the landscape in his spare time to look for archaeological materials of the Roman period. Since many Roman coins had been found in the area north of Osnabrück, Schlüter told Clunn that the locale might be a good one to investigate. Clunn worked in close collaboration with Schlüter and his colleagues, reporting his finds to them regularly and jointly planning his ongoing research. After studying maps and records about earlier finds made in the area that Schlüter had recommended, Clunn chose a location where he thought it likely that he would find what he was after. Searching near the spot where a boy had found a Roman coin in 1963, over the course of a few weeks in July and August of 1987, he found remains of the battle that had taken place there 1,978 years before—the battle that resulted in many profound changes for the young Roman Empire.

But those first discoveries of coins and of a lead surveying weight did not clinch the link between the archaeological objects and the great battle. The ancient Germanic tribes of this region had traded intensively with the Roman world, and thousands of Roman coins, pots, bronze vessels, pieces of jewelry, and other items have been found on their settlements and in their graves. Yet already the coins were raising suspicions. Like the overwhelming majority of the coins found by farmers in the region, many of which had been amassed into a collection of many hundreds by the local landowning von Bar family, they had all been minted before the end of the reign of the Roman emperor

Augustus, in A.D. 14. As Clunn continued his search, both by studying maps and in the field, through the winter of 1987–88 and into the spring of 1988, he found more coins and numerous fragments of lead and of bronze.

Suddenly one day, the discovery of three lead objects roughly the size and shape of robin's eggs changed the picture. Schlüter recognized these as slingstones, the first evidence that all of the accumulating Roman finds were linked not to trade but to military activity (see illustration 4). Slingstones made of lead (such as these three), stone, or baked clay, were important weapons in the Roman military and among some of its enemies until the second century A.D. Most soldiers probably received some training in use of the sling, though there were also specialist slingers associated with some units. The stones were hurled with a leather sling that the soldier whirled around his head before letting go of one end. Enemies dreaded the sling, because the projectiles flew so fast that they were not visible as they approached, and they could do horrific damage, even to a soldier wearing armor. Their accurate range in the hands of skilled slingers was up to two hundred yards.

Roman military activity eighty-five miles northeast of the imperial frontier on the Rhine, dated by the hundreds of coins at not later than A.D. 14, could mean only one thing: after six hundred years of searching, the site of the Battle of the Teutoburg Forest had been found.

Through the subsequent intensive investigations directed by Wolfgang Schlüter, archaeological remains of the battle have been recovered over an area about four by three miles in what is known as the Kalkriese-Niewedde Depression. The site is bounded on the south by the 350-foot high Kalkriese Hill, a northward extension of the Wiehengebirge range, and on the north by damp, low-lying lands that include a large bog complex known as the Great Bog (see map 3). The largest concentration of archaeological finds so far has been along the southern edge of the hourglass-shaped parcel of land about half a mile wide at its

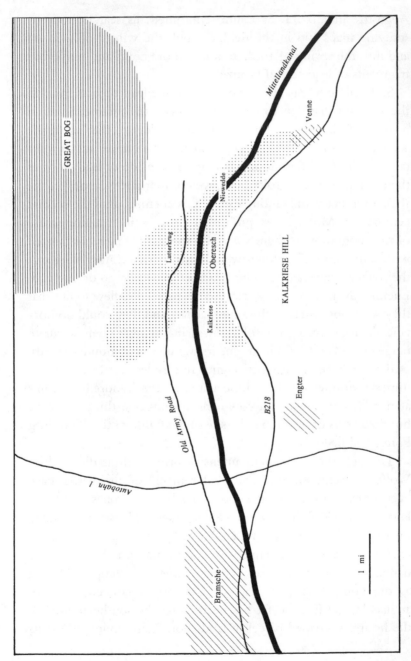

Map 3. Map showing the battle site in the Kalkriese-Niewedde Depression and physical features around it. The modern city of Bramsche and the villages of Engter and Venne are indicated by oblique hatching. The area of densest concentration of Roman finds on the site is shown by shading.

narrowest between the hill and the bog. The brooks that flow northward down the slope of the Kalkriese Hill and across the low-lying land into the Great Bog create narrow, often deep valleys that made passage difficult before modern landscaping.

Until the modern lowering of the water table, only the southern and northern edges of the half-mile-wide gap between the Kalkriese Hill and the Great Bog were easily passable, along deposits of sand that offered more or less dry footing above the surrounding sodden sediments. In places, these sandy deposits were only some one hundred yards wide. Until the B218 highway was built in 1845 along the southern edge of the pass, the main road went along the northern sand ridge, where modern maps still label the route the Old Army Road. But many prehistoric finds, as well as the locations of historic farms, indicate that early traffic moved along the southern edge of the pass as well.

Excavations at Kalkriese

The place where a Roman coin was found in 1963 and where in 1987 Tony Clunn recovered a scattered hoard of 160 silver denarii and three glass game pieces is known as Lutterkrug, situated on the Old Army Road. Following Clunn's discoveries in the summer of 1987, Wolfgang Schlüter organized a systematic survey that included both surface collection and use of a metal detector to explore fields, meadows, and forested areas in the Kalkriese-Niewedde Depression. Between 1987 and 1992, about three-fourths of a square mile was surveyed in this fashion, one-fifth of the total area of the depression. Objects dating from the late Stone Age to the present were recovered. They included, in addition to the 160 silver coins and three glass objects found by Clunn, 135 Roman coins (1 gold, 48 silver, and 86 copper) and twenty-nine other objects associated with the Roman military.

In September 1989, systematic excavations began on the land

known as the Oberesch, a part of the sand ridge along the base of the Kalkriese Hill that farmers had built up over the centuries with turf and compost. With brooks crossing parts of it and other portions low and boggy, only about half of the Oberesch was dry land before the recent in-filling. On those dry areas, the archaeologists found remains of human habitation from the late Stone Age to the late Iron Age. Studies of the soil indicate that it was open farmland at the time of the battle. In addition to uncovering a great many Roman military objects here, the excavations revealed something completely unexpected.

The Wall

At the base of the slope of the Kalkriese Hill, just north of the modern highway, the excavators found remains of a wall built of sod. At its base, the wall was about fifteen feet wide. Excavations have revealed over two thousand feet of its length, extending east–west along the base of the slope. The excavators estimate that the wall was around five feet high, and in places a wooden fence stood on top. Part of the wall had a facing of limestone blocks. A ditch at the base of the uphill side of the wall may have served to channel water that ran down the slope during rain, allowing it to flow through passages in the wall and down the slope into the Great Bog. Many Roman objects have been found in the ditch, indicating that it was open at the time of the battle.

The surprising discovery of this wall suggests that the German warriors who ambushed the Roman legions had constructed this elaborate defensive work well in advance of the arrival of the Roman marching column. Apparently the ambush had been planned carefully. Constructed at the base of the forested slope, along the relatively dry sandbank on which the Roman soldiers would be marching, this wall provided both camouflage cover and military protection for the attackers. Warriors may have crouched behind the wall, hidden from sight at the edge of the woods, until the moment of the attack, and they could have used the wall as protection as they launched their weapons against the marching legionaries.

Exceptionally large quantities of Roman military objects and of bone fragments have been recovered in front of the wall. Several objects considerably larger than most of the fragmentary weapons were found immediately in front of it. These include a silver-covered iron face mask, catapult bolt points, a pickax, sickles, and parts of helmets. The excavators believe that a portion of the wall collapsed during the battle, covering weapons that had fallen right in front of it. The reason that large objects have not been discovered all over the battlefield is that the victorious German warriors scoured the field to collect usable weapons and tools. They took swords, daggers, lances, spears, helmets, shields, and other weapons to use themselves, to trade, or to forge into other objects. Another theory to explain the large objects near the front of the wall is that they were left, or intentionally placed, there as part of a ritual deposit created on the battlefield by the victors (see chapter 10).

The Roman Weapons

The clearest indication of what happened at this place nearly two thousand years ago is the great quantity of fragmentary Roman weapons that the archaeologists are recovering. As of the end of 1999, investigations at Kalkriese yielded over 4,000 Roman objects, including about 3,100 military items and 1,160 coins. (Finds made before 1987 include 205 objects, all but one of them coins.) Except for glass game pieces, glass beads, three glass eyes from statues, and some sherds of pottery, all of the objects are metal. The principal categories are weapons, clothing paraphernalia, personal ornaments, equipment associated with cavalry horses and wagon-pulling mules, tools, and coins. With the exception of coins, all of the objects are of a distinctly military rather than civilian character. Similar objects are well represented at the Roman military bases in the Rhineland and on the Lippe, such as Haltern (see chapter 5). Very few of the weapons recovered are intact, and those are small ones, such as spearheads and slingstones. This pattern of many fragmentary weapons but very few complete ones is typical for a battlefield that was plundered.

Long-range projectile weapons recovered include slingstones, arrowheads, catapult bolt points (see illustration 5), parts of javelins (illustration 6), and spearpoints. Among weapons used in hand-to-hand combat were fragments of swords, daggers, and scabbards. Defensive weapons include remains of helmets, such as iron supports for the crests on top of officers' helmets, a bronze knob from the top of another, and a complete cheekpiece from another helmet. Large numbers of iron nails from the legionaries' hobnailed boots have been found. Horses and mules—the cavalry mounts and the draft animals of the legions—are represented both by their bones (see below) and by metal objects that formed parts of their harnesses. (For more details about the Roman weapons recovered on the battle site, see appendix 2.)

Besides weapons, Roman legionaries carried a wide range of tools for a variety of purposes. The finds at Kalkriese include pickaxes (see illustration 7), hammers, lead plumb bobs used in surveying (illustration 8), chisels for working wood, awls for processing leather, surgical instruments (illustration 9), shears, razors, keys, locks, lead weights, and a fragmentary scale.

An iron stylus for writing on wax tablets was found. Four bronze seal boxes were recovered. The three with intact lids were decorated with unusually ornate lead relief figures. These boxes, like the silver trim on weapons noted above, represent officers of rank. Seal boxes were used to secure documents encased in wooden frames. The frames were tied together with string, and the binding sealed by the sender. The seal box protected the seal from tampering while the document was in transit.

Remains of bronze casseroles represent the standard food-preparing equipment of the Roman soldier. Other bronze vessels, such as wine strainers, cauldrons, buckets, and basins, attest to beverage preparation and service, perhaps among the troops, perhaps for officers. But a silver spoon and the handle of a silver bowl represent the dining equipment of officers. Three glass eyes from statues also represent possessions of officers—perhaps of the commander himself; they may have been sculptures from decorative furniture.

Glass game pieces are common on Roman military sites and bespeak a regular pastime among soldiers. Large numbers have been found at Kalkriese. A lead die represents another game of chance that soldiers enjoyed playing.

A small number of objects may indicate the presence of women with the troops (see illustration 10). A hairpin, a disk brooch, and a butterfly brooch are jewelry items characteristically worn by women. It is conceivable that a woman gave a personal ornament to a soldier, so we cannot conclude from these three objects that women were there. Additional finds would strengthen the evidence for the presence of women, supporting Cassius Dio's assertion that women and children accompanied Varus and his army.

While Roman weapons are abundant on the site, matching standard legionary and auxiliary equipment, weapons characteristic of the local people—Arminius's warriors—are sparse. An iron spur is one of the few distinctively non-Roman objects. This dearth of clearly German weapons is not surprising, when we consider the way the archaeological site was formed and the character of German military gear.

First, after the battle, when the winners collected the usable Roman weapons, they also collected all of the weapons of their fallen comrades. Second, although they probably used some of

the Roman weapons to form a ritual deposit on the site, perhaps
as a trophy display (see chapter 10), they did not use any of their
own weapons in that way. Everything we know about the ritual
weapon deposits in northern Europe indicates that weapons of
defeated enemies were offered, but not those of victors. Third,
many of Arminius's men probably used Roman-made weapons,
indistinguishable from those carried by the legionaries. Arminius
and others had served as auxiliaries with the Roman army, and
they likely acquired Roman arms. Thus some of the weapons
recovered on the site may have been used by the German fighters, but we cannot distinguish them. Fourth, the German
warriors did not wear as many metal ornaments as Roman
legionaries did. The Roman soldiers wore metal ornaments on
their belts, tunics, and various leather straps. These ornaments are
among the most numerous objects recovered at Kalkriese.

Human and Animal Bones

For reasons cited above, we would not expect large numbers of
bones to survive on a battlefield. Corpses, including bones,
would be consumed by animals, and human bodies might be
buried by survivors. But important deposits of bones have come
to light in the course of the Kalkriese excavations. Many small
fragments of human bones are reported from the surface, especially in front of the wall on the Oberesch. Complete human and
animal bones have been recovered in five pits on the Oberesch.
These were burials not of intact corpses but of disarticulated
bones that were collected from the surface and placed in the pits.
Since these bone deposits represent postbattle activity and not
battlefield action, I discuss them in chapter 10. All of the human
bones that have been analyzed are those of young adult and adult
males, and some have cut marks indicating a death caused by
sharp weapons. Among the animal bones, investigators have identified remains of at least eight horses and thirty mules.

Remains of two mules that were found on the battlefield surface rather than in the pits are particularly important. Underneath the collapsed wall were the skull, neck, and shoulder bones of a mule, together with parts of its harness, including an iron bit and chain. With them were a bronze pendant of a type often placed around draft animals' necks and a large bronze bell with an iron clapper. The bell had been stuffed full of straw from oats and peas. Someone had torn the plants from the ground (small roots remained attached) and stuffed them into the bell to silence it. Could the mule driver have done this to avoid attracting attention, or to dampen extraneous noise so that the troops could hear sounds in the woods? The stage of growth of the plants shows that they were torn from the ground in late summer or early autumn, matching the September date of the battle.

In 1999 an almost complete skeleton of a four-year-old female mule was found close to the wall on the Oberesch (see illustration 11). With it was a bronze bell, smaller than the bell with the first mule, and an iron bit. This animal died of a broken neck. Perhaps, in the panic of the battle, the animal tried to scramble over the wall, fell, and broke its neck.

Such dramatic discoveries continue at the site as archaeologists carry on their excavations at Kalkriese. These discoveries, together with the Roman accounts, allow us to reconstruct what probably happened at this place almost two millennia ago.

4
AUGUSTUS:
ROME'S FIRST EMPEROR

As the soldiers of Rome's Seventeenth, Eighteenth, and Nineteenth Legions lay dead or dying in the mud and marshland pools of the north, and as dusk fell on the gloomy wilderness of this deadly trap for overconfident Romans, a completely different scene was playing out in the imperial capital seven hundred miles to the south.

Life in Rome in A.D. 9

In the warm September evening, the workday was drawing to a close for hundreds of thousands of Romans. All along the side streets, merchants were closing up their storefronts for the night, and the crowds of customers were dwindling. Women were hurrying home with their baskets of fruits and vegetables to prepare the evening meal for their families, since their husbands would arrive shortly. In the markets, farmers were packing up the remains of the produce they had brought into the city before dawn and beginning to drive their creaky wagons through the streets, out the city gates, and back to their farms. It would be several days before the emperor Augustus learned of the catastrophe in the north, and even longer before the Roman citizens grasped its meaning for the future of their city and the lands it ruled.

Rome was the largest city in the world in A.D. 9, with a population of around a million people. In the center were broad boulevards paved with stone, lined with stone and brick buildings, and with gleaming marble temples, palaces, forums, and other public monuments sponsored by rich men, especially by the emperor Augustus himself. Huge columned temples honored the Roman gods, such as Jupiter and Mars, and over-life-size statues glorified the city's human heroes. Much of Rome's center was new, and in A.D. 9 many construction projects were under way. Augustus had carried out a massive program of renewal, tearing down old buildings and erecting new ones in their place, and he was especially active in building public monuments to the glory of Rome and its rulers. He is said to have boasted, "I arrived in a city of brick, and I created a city of marble." Among the major public buildings he had erected were the Forum of Augustus (considerably larger than the forum Julius Caesar had built in 46 B.C.), the Theater of Marcellus (named for his nephew), the Baths of Agrippa (named for a loyal follower who had served as governor of Gaul), the Pantheon, the Altar of Peace (Ara Pacis), the enormous sundial (*horologium*) that included an Egyptian carved stone obelisk as pointer, and his own imposing burial monument, the Mausoleum of Augustus.

As in every major city—such as New York, Washington, Paris, and London today—outside of the grandiose center, the streets and neighborhoods were much more modest. In a few parts of Rome, there were magnificent brick and stone residences of the wealthy, while much of the city was occupied by multistory apartment buildings made of concrete faced with brick, where the majority of the inhabitants lived. A law passed under Augustus's reign restricted the height of such structures to sixty feet, allowing five stories, but it was not always obeyed.

In the business and market areas, the Roman streets were bustling all day and well into the warm Mediterranean evenings. In the markets, farmers arrived from the fields outside the city to offer their fruits, vegetables, and meats to hungry city dwellers. Small shops along the streets housed jewelers, weavers, wood-carvers, and all manner of other crafts workers. Laborers and slaves bustled along the edges of the streets on their errands.

Roman society was highly stratified. At the top of the social pyramid stood the emperor Augustus and his family—his wife, Livia, his surviving adopted son, Tiberius, and a variety of nieces, nephews, and younger offspring. His only child, Julia, had by this time been banished from Rome for her outrageous behavior, as we will see below. Next in rank were the senators, some six hundred men from Rome's richest and most distinguished families, their wealth and status deriving mainly from extensive landholdings. Filling out the bottom part of the elite were members of the eques-trian class, or knights. They too were rich men. Many of the officials who administered the city and went abroad as provincial governors, and many officers in the army, came from the equestrian class. Below this upper part of the social pyramid were the free citizens of Rome—crafts workers, merchants, sailors, and other laborers and, in the countryside beyond the city limits, farmers.

At the bottom of the hierarchy were slaves, persons either cap-tured in battle or seized from a defeated populace, or children of persons already enslaved. Most slaves stemmed not from either Italy or Greece but from other lands conquered by the Roman army. Life for slaves varied greatly, depending upon the treatment they received from their owners and the jobs they were required to do. Some slaves worked on farms, others in factories making pottery, others as domestic servants in the homes of the wealthy. In A.D. 9, Rome may have had as many as 200,000 slaves among its million people. Slaves were often permitted to acquire wealth, and many bought their freedom, became citizens, and, some-times, even became extremely wealthy. Finally, by this time Rome had considerable numbers of foreigners in residence, mostly from different parts of the Empire but also from beyond it. Gauls, Greeks, Syrians, and North Africans contributed to the rich diversity of languages, religious beliefs, and traditions of this huge and cosmopolitan city.

All of the important offices in the Roman government were held by wealthy men. Women were in charge of their households, and wealthy women could often wield considerable power, particularly if their husbands were senators or the emperor. Some important ritual roles were held by women, such as those of the vestal virgins, who were responsible for tending the sacred fire of Rome. In this special position, they often exercised appreciable political power.

Wealthy Romans lived in big houses. Each had a sizable front door opening onto the street, a spacious entrance hall, and rows of rooms that surrounded a courtyard that was open to the air, usually with a fountain and beds of flowers. Floors of some rooms had mosaics that formed patterns or pictures, and the walls of many rooms were colorfully painted with outdoor scenery. The great majority of the Roman populace inhabited apartment houses that were typically four or five stories high and situated on narrow, crowded streets. Families lived in small, cramped, and poorly lit and ventilated rooms without running water and often without cooking facilities.

Wealthy Romans spent part of each day at the baths, which played a role in some ways similar to that of social clubs in modern America. After their business of the day was complete, affluent men went off to the baths to meet other elites, to relax in the steam baths or swim in the pools, to conduct casual business, chat, and perhaps play friendly games of dice. Other Romans could also go to the public baths, but many had no spare time for such activities. Water for the baths, like that for general use, was supplied by a system of aqueducts that brought abundant fresh water from hilly regions outside of Rome into the urban center. Many wealthy Romans had conduits that brought water directly into their homes, while poorer persons had to use public fountains to collect the water they needed.

Day-to-day life in Rome was enlivened by regular festivals, such as Lupercalia and Saturnalia, that were celebrated by a large proportion of the population. Festivals had a religious basis and served to maintain the favor of the gods. For many festivals, state officials carried out rituals at temples dedicated to the major Roman deities. But it was the public games that generated the most enthusiasm. Besides the events put on by the city, wealthy individuals often sponsored public spectacles to win favor from the Roman populace. Elites and commoners alike enjoyed the games sponsored by the emperor or other wealthy Romans, often to celebrate and draw attention to particular events, especially victorious military campaigns. Chariot races, staged fights between wild animals, brought from as far away as Africa, and gladiatorial contests delighted the mass of Rome's population, including the emperor Augustus. Augustus's biographer Suetonius notes that unlike Julius Caesar, who was sometimes observed reading letters during games he attended, Augustus gave the spectacles his full attention.

Gladiators tended to be criminals or slaves. They were specially trained for their public performances, and their battles were organized with great care with regard to the weapons and tactics they could use. The first stone amphitheater in Rome, called the Amphitheater of Satillus Taurus, was constructed during Augustus's reign, and this is where the gladiatorial fights were held. (The famous Colosseum was not built until about seventy years after his death.)

Romans honored a number of different gods and spirits. The head of the Roman pantheon was Jupiter, and Rome maintained an official state cult in his honor. But people worshiped many other deities as well, including prominent official gods such as Venus and Mars, and spirits of individual houses and of natural forces. Worshiping gods involved making sacrifices, which could take the form of killing an animal and burning parts of it on an altar dedicated to a specific god, or tossing offerings of coins, jewelry, or pottery into sacred places as dedications to the deity. Huge ornate temples in the city honored the principal official gods, and small altars were common in people's houses for honoring spirits that were special to individual households.

The diet of Romans in A.D. 9 was unlike what we think of as Italian food today. Pasta did not exist in Italy at the time, and the tomato was unknown until it was brought to Europe from South America in the sixteenth century. The Roman diet consisted mainly of grains, legumes, olive oil, and wine. Wheat, the principal staple, was often cooked with water to make a porridge or baked into bread. Lentils, beans, peas, cabbage, onions, radishes, and lettuce supplied important nutrients and lent some variety to the diet. Only the wealthy were able to eat meat often. The poor had to be content with a small piece once every few days.

Well-to-do Romans had access to all kinds of delicacies, both locally produced and imported. From the sea came shellfish, especially oysters, and fish. Dormice and snails were considered special fare, and domestic as well as wild birds were much favored. Different kinds of cakes sweetened with honey were popular after meals. The wealthy enjoyed olives and nuts of different kinds. Spices and herbs were imported from all parts of the provinces and beyond to grace the tables and delight the palates of the rich. Romans everywhere were particularly fond of a sauce called *garum*, made from fermented fish, probably something like modern Worcestershire sauce. Many liked to sprinkle this pungent flavoring over a wide variety of foods, and *garum* was a major trade commodity, shipped throughout the Roman world in large ceramic amphoras, just as wine and olive oil were transported. Romans did not have forks. They ate with their hands and sometimes with spoons.

Rome's poor received monthly allotments of wheat. During his reign, Augustus oversaw the doling out of grain to some 200,000 of the city's poorest citizens, and he supervised the supply of adequate fresh water delivered by the system of aqueducts.

Rome's Ruler in A.D. 9

Augustus, the man who ruled over this enormous and complex city, at the center of the greatest empire of the ancient world, was seventy-two years old in A.D. 9. He was unique in Roman, and indeed world, history. His given name at birth was Octavius, and the Roman Senate bestowed upon him the honorific name Augustus in 27 B.C. As Rome's first emperor, he established many precedents for his successors to follow during the four centuries after his rule. After two decades of calamitous civil wars, Augustus restored peace and harmony to Roman Italy, and he presided over forty-five years of prosperity and civil order. He organized the Roman army as the professional fighting force that guaranteed the might of the Empire. He was an almost unimaginably powerful and wealthy man, for more than four decades supreme ruler of an empire that encircled the Mediterranean Sea and included half of Europe, Africa north of the Sahara Desert, and most of the Near East.

Augustus the Man

The man who was to become Rome's first emperor was born on September 23, 63 B.C. Like his father, he was named Gaius Octavius. He was born in Rome, but his father hailed from Velitrae, in the Alban Hills, twenty-five miles southeast of the city. The family of the elder Gaius Octavius belonged to the equestrian class of Roman Italy. His grandfather had served as a town official and may have worked as a money changer. The family thus had status as equestrians and possessed at least some wealth, but was not one of the old elite families of Roman tradition. Augustus's father was the first member of the family to attain the rank of senator. Through his energy and determination, he had become a member of the Roman Senate and was elected to the office of praetor—a magistrate of the city of Rome—in 61 B.C. In the years 61–59, he served successfully as governor of Macedonia. Shortly after returning to Rome, he died suddenly, leaving his son and two daughters fatherless.

Young Octavius's mother, Atia, on the other hand, provided the boy with a highly influential pedigree. Atia was the daughter of Atius Balbus, who came from northern Africa, and of Julia. Julia was the sister of Julius Caesar, an increasingly powerful politician. This family connection played a vital role in young Octavius's rise to prominence and power in late Republican Rome.

We are not well informed about Octavius's childhood. Since, unlike his great uncle, he was not a member of one of Rome's most elite families, chroniclers of the time did not follow the course of his early education. And in his later years, Augustus was reticent about his personal life and said little concerning his upbringing. The Julii family, to which Julius Caesar belonged, was one of the most distinguished and powerful in Republican Rome, and young Octavius's own immediate family must have made him very much aware of this connection and of the ongoing achievements of his great-uncle.

An important event is recorded from the year 51 B.C., when Octavius was twelve. At the funeral ceremony for Julia, his grandmother, Octavius gave an oration in her honor. We do not know the content of that speech, but it is likely that he drew attention to the Julii family's contributions to Rome and in particular to the recent success of Julia's brother, Julius Caesar, in conquering Gaul, adding that huge and rich territory to Rome's domain. Funerals were occasions on which families displayed their status and importance, and this event was probably Octavius's initiation into active politics. When Octavius was fifteen, he was honored by being granted the privilege of wearing the *toga virilis*—the garment of the elite adult male—a privilege usually first conferred upon young men at the age of seventeen.

Octavius's relationship with his great-uncle was a formative factor in his development as a self-confident and ambitious young man and later in his rise to the supreme power in Rome.

Julius Caesar and His Great-Nephew Octavius

The years between 120 and 60 B.C. had been a time of immense change in Rome. From the middle of the first millennium B.C. on, Rome grew rapidly from a modest town in central Italy to the great and expansive power that dominated the whole central Mediterranean region (map 4). As a result of Rome's early conquests of Sicily, part of Iberia, Illyria, Asia Minor, Macedonia, Greece, and parts of North Africa, great riches accrued to the city's powerful families and stress between the wealthy and the mass of Rome's population increased. In the social, political, and economic struggles, unusual power came into the hands of a few individuals. In the first half of the first century B.C., four main competitors vied for supreme power in Rome—Marius, Sulla, Pompey, and Caesar.

In 58 B.C., Julius Caesar led his legions into Gaul (see chapter 7). According to his own detailed written account, the purpose was to aid tribes there allied with Rome that requested assistance in repelling incursions by the Helvetii and the Suebi, local tribal groups. The circumstances of Caesar's decision to intervene in Gaul are murky, and recently scholars have argued that he may actually have provoked the conflicts and used them as justifications for his military campaigns there. In the course of eight years of fighting, Caesar led his legions to successful conquest of the whole of Gaul, from the Pyrenees to the Rhine. Throughout these years, he was increasingly engaged in struggles with his powerful rivals in Rome. When Caesar took his legions southward across the Rubicon River into central Italy in 49 B.C., he precipitated civil war between the rival factions. After fighting in

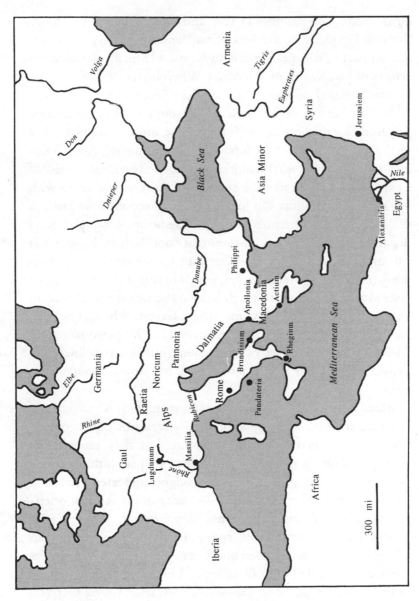

Map 4. Map showing places mentioned in chapter 4 and subsequent chapters.

49–47 against his enemies in Italy and Greece, he led his troops through Egypt, Syria, and Asia Minor, lending military and political support to regimes friendly to Rome. He finally defeated the armies of his rivals in North Africa. When he returned to Rome, he was honored with grand triumphal celebrations.

In the course of his military adventures, Caesar became involved in a relationship with one of the most influential rulers in the ancient world, Cleopatra (see illustration 12). After arriving with his army at Alexandria on the Mediterranean coast of Egypt in 48 B.C., he met Cleopatra, and he remained there with her for several months. On June 23 of 47, Cleopatra gave birth to their son, whom she named Ptolemy Caesarion. Although Caesar departed from Egypt on business that took him to Rome, Asia Minor, Syria, and Africa, his affair with Cleopatra served to bolster her hold on power in Egypt, which in turn helped assure that taxes would flow from this rich land to the treasury at Rome. In 46, Cleopatra traveled to Rome, where Caesar, although married to Calpurnia, treated her and her husband as his personal guests. The visit had the effect of strengthening friendly political ties between Egypt and Rome, which were to remain important for both.

Meanwhile, Caesar favored his great-nephew Octavius and arranged for him to be appointed to a series of public offices. These were largely honorific in nature, but they brought the young man into public view and helped prepare him for future political office. In 47 B.C., Caesar strongly supported Octavius's election to the office of pontifex—a leader in the Roman priesthood—and had him appointed city prefect. Later Caesar arranged for Octavius to be appointed, at only eighteen years of age, to the highly regarded office of *magister equitum*—master of the horse, a mainly honorific office that included both command of cavalry forces and direct assistance to Caesar. Young Octavius frequently accompanied Caesar around Rome, as part of his entourage, to political events and social functions, an association from which the rising young Roman was to benefit in future years.

In 45 B.C., Octavius traveled to Spain to join Caesar on campaign there, gaining some early direct military experience. Later that year, Caesar arranged to have Octavius go to Apollonia, on the east coast of the Adriatic Sea, for further education. One reason for Caesar's selection of Apollonia may have been that five Roman legions were stationed in Macedonia, affording Octavius the opportunity to continue to learn military ways along with the rest of his schooling.

In February of the year 44, in gratitude for the victories he won for Rome and for a certain stability he brought to the city after the chaos of the civil wars, officials and the people of Rome appointed Caesar dictator in perpetuity. He further succeeded, after some effort, in having the Roman Senate honor him as a god. The power he was amassing frightened many among Rome's elites, and a group of senators conspired to murder Julius Caesar on the Ides of March—March 15, 44 B.C.

Octavius's Rise to Power

Upon hearing of Caesar's death, Octavius sailed from Apollonia to Brundisium, in southern Italy. There he learned from allies that in his will written the year before, Caesar, having no legitimate children of his own, had legally adopted Octavius and made him his heir. Since Caesar had many enemies in Roman Italy, and since Octavius could count on their striving to limit his ability to assume his great-uncle's mantle, he proceeded cautiously in claiming his inheritance. Through the adoption by Caesar, Octavius had now become a member of the highly distinguished Julii family, and he could assume the name Julius Caesar Octavianus. Furthermore, since his adoptive father had been officially deified before his death,

Octavius—from this point known as Octavian—could also use the title *Divi Julii filius*—son of the god Julius (Caesar).

Octavian waited a couple of months in southern Italy and in Campania, talking with supporters to learn how volatile the political situation was, before returning to Rome. When he finally arrived in Rome in May as the returning adopted son of Caesar, according to reports a halo seen around the sun was interpreted as a positive omen. From this point on, Octavian became engaged in a long struggle between leaders who claimed to represent the murdered Caesar. Octavian's principal stated aim was the avenging of Caesar's death. When the people of Rome elected him to the office of consul—one of two civil and military magistrates of the city, in effect the two supreme rulers of the Roman world, elected annually—the appearance of twelve vultures flying overhead was understood as another omen, this one linking Octavian with the legendary founder of Rome, Romulus. Octavian was still only nineteen years old.

For a decade, beginning in 43 B.C., three powerful men—Octavian, Mark Antony, and M. Aemilius Lepidus—agreed to band together as a triumvirate to confront their common enemies, in the process executing or banishing hundreds of political opponents. In 42 B.C. at Philippi, in Macedonia, they defeated the armies of Brutus and Cassius, the leaders of the conspiracy against Caesar that had resulted in his assassination. Back in Italy, they confiscated lands to reward the soldiers who had fought for them; this created further chaos, disruption, and fear throughout Roman Italy.

After Lepidus lost the confidence of his army and thus his ability to rival Octavian and Antony, the competition for supreme power over Rome was reduced to two men. From early on in his quest for power, Octavian understood the importance of the support of his army, and as the heir of Caesar he was given strong backing by both the veterans and the populace of Rome. In preparation for an engagement with Mark Antony's forces in their rivalry for the role of Caesar's successor, Octavian paid his soldiers 2,500 denarii each from the Roman treasury, about ten times their annual salary.

Antony and Cleopatra

In order to strengthen his position as a contender for sole rule of Rome, Antony planned a major military campaign against the Parthian Empire, Rome's principal competition on the eastern frontier. The Parthians, who occupied the region of modern Iraq and Iran, were a formidable political power and military force at this time, known particularly for their fierce cavalry and skilled archers. In earlier fighting, Parthian forces had captured Roman legionary eagles. To establish a base for supplies to support this initiative, Antony decided to approach Cleopatra of Egypt. The resulting arrangement was highly advantageous to Cleopatra. It reaffirmed her position as queen of Egypt and provided her with a direct connection to one of Rome's two current rulers. Antony and Cleopatra began a romantic relationship, and in the fall of 40 B.C. Cleopatra gave birth to twins, a girl and a boy. At the time, Antony was in Rome marrying Octavian's sister Octavia, in an attempt to build an alliance with his rival. But that political alliance did not last long.

In 37 B.C. Antony left Octavia and Italy to rejoin Cleopatra. A year later, his first major campaign against the Parthians ended in a Roman defeat. In January of 35, Cleopatra bore another child by Antony. The following year, Antony conducted more success-ful military operations against the Parthians, achieving a victory that he celebrated grandly in Alexandria. Meanwhile in Rome, Octavian mounted a public campaign against Antony, enlisting the Senate to turn against him. On September 2, 31, Octavian led his navy against the combined naval forces of Antony and Cleopatra off Actium, in western Greece, winning a major victory. Finally in the summer of 30, Octavian's army attacked and defeated the remaining forces of Antony and Cleopatra in Egypt. In the end, Antony and Cleopatra both committed suicide, and Octavian had Cleopatra's son by Caesar, Caesarion, killed to remove him as a possible contender for power. Octavian did not order the deaths of her three children fathered by Antony.

Octavian/Augustus Becomes Sole Ruler of Rome

In order to gain an important political connection with one of Rome's leading families, Octavian had in 40 B.C. married a woman named Scribonia. She was related by marriage to Sextus Pompeius, a powerful political and military leader whose support Octavian wanted in his rivalry with Antony. Octavian divorced Scribonia in the following year, apparently on the very day that Scribonia gave birth to their daughter Julia, who was Octavian's only legitimate child. On January 17, 38, Octavian married Livia Drusilla, a clever and crafty nineteen-year-old woman with powerful political connections, who divorced her husband in order to marry Octavian. Her son Tiberius was three years old at the time, and her other son, Drusus, had been born just three days before her marriage with Octavian. These two boys were to become Augustus's principal generals in his wars against the Germans.

The new union provided Octavian with a link to the Claudii, another old and powerful family in Republican Rome. At about this same time, Octavian assumed the title Imperator Caesar to convey his leadership of the political group in Rome that claimed to be the political heirs of Caesar. He also commissioned the construction of his mausoleum—an enormous circular burial monument built of stone, 130 feet high and 285 feet in diameter—near the center of the city of Rome. The main reason why the twenty-five-year-old Octavian wanted such a monument was probably to create a powerful visual sign of his status and authority to serve him in his struggle for power with Antony. Throughout his often ruthless dealings with friends and enemies alike, Octavian consistently portrayed himself as the defender of Roman tradition and in particular as the restorer of the Republic—a period remembered for its relative peace in Italy and higher morals among Romans.

Octavian's defeat of Antony and Cleopatra at the Battle of Actium ended the rivalry for power in Rome in Octavian's favor and opened the way for the incorporation of Egypt into the Roman Empire as a province in 30 B.C. In the next year, Octavian returned to Rome as a great hero, to celebrate a grand triumph for his victories. He now began his extensive program of public building throughout the city. Much of the construction was truly monumental, intended to display to the citizens of the city the power, history, and traditions of Rome. It included statuary, religious buildings, and practical structures such as aqueducts to provide the city with clean water for its baths, as well as for drinking and cooking.

In the year 27 B.C., Octavian was accorded near-absolute power by Roman officials and the people. On January 16, the Roman Senate granted him the title Augustus, a name that conveyed the meanings "dignified" and "sacred." The Senate named the sixth month of the Roman calendar "Augustus" in his honor, a name preserved today in many languages for what is our eighth month. Between 27 and 13 B.C., Augustus, as he was now called, spent the majority of his time outside of Rome in the imperial territories, overseeing the administration of the provinces and organizing for future conquests along the frontiers. He was now the commander in chief of all of Rome's armies, a position for which he was well qualified, having distinguished himself in battles during the 40s and 30s. He had commanded successful naval operations off Sicily and at Actium, and was close to the action in land campaigns in Dalmatia and Cantabria. In Dalmatia, he was wounded, struck on the leg by a slingstone. In numerous other engagements, he let his generals oversee the combat, but he assumed responsibility for overall strategy.

In order to maintain a standing army of sufficient size and to keep morale of the soldiers high, Augustus frequently paid them from his own resources. He was by far the wealthiest person in the Roman world, and he used his personal wealth not only to pay active troops but also to provide settlements for veterans after their service, to erect public buildings in Rome, to sponsor games, and to aid financially troubled individuals. Even after expending hundreds of millions of sestertii on the army and various public works, when he died in A.D. 14, Augustus left some 250 million sestertii to his heirs, the army, and the Roman people. The sources of his vast wealth were many—inheritance from his father and from his great-uncle Julius Caesar, gifts from wealthy Romans, war booty from his conquests, and tribute payments of various sorts from the provinces.

Augustus began to organize a widespread system of taxation for the entire Empire. Specific forms of taxes and collection varied in different regions, but in general two main types of taxes were collected in the provinces—a poll tax that every adult had to pay, and a tax on assets such as land and houses. Careful censuses of the population and assessments of landholdings were carried out to assure a reasonably equitable collection of taxes. Under Augustus, taxes were not so high that any part of the population suffered much, though under later emperors the peasant farmers did not fare so well. At the borders of the Empire, customs duties were collected, and smaller duties had to be paid on goods transported between provinces. Finally, Augustus levied an inheritance tax on the citizens of Rome. Proceeds of the various taxes and duties were destined for Augustus at the center of the Roman system. In some parts of the Empire, there was vigorous public resistance to the imposition of taxes. Tax collection and the bureaucratic process of which it was part played major roles in creating dissatisfaction among peoples in many of Rome's provinces.

Under Augustus, the Roman legions were active in conquering new territories, especially in Europe, and in regularly winning glory for Rome (see illustration 13). This military activity served a number of purposes. It increased Augustus's power and influence greatly, assuring him the continued support of the army and of the Roman people. The more or less continual warfare provided the rationale for Augustus to maintain a large standing army that he could rely on in case any new leaders were to contest his supremacy. Newly conquered territories were lands upon which Augustus could settle veterans. And, of course, the conquests provided new tax revenues for him and his administration. He and his supporters took full advantage of the idea that Roman armies could conquer the whole world, though it is likely that at least on some level Augustus knew that the propaganda to that effect was misleading. In fact, his policy along the frontiers was to establish friendly and mutually beneficial relations with leaders of groups on the other side of Rome's provincial borders. This policy served to maintain some degree of peace along most of the frontiers and to create a buffer between the Roman lands and more distant peoples who might launch invasions into the rich provinces.

Augustus saw to it that the people of Rome were well cared for. Besides assuring consistent water and food supplies, he commissioned the numerous temples, statues, and other public works that demonstrated the power and wealth of the city and provided the people with visual reminders of Rome's glory and of the values he was trying to convey. He took special pains to emphasize the continuity of tradition from the Republic, with the celebration of religious rituals and public festivals that re-created the old Roman traditions. On January 11, 29 B.C., the doors to the temple of Janus in the Roman Forum were closed, symbolizing that Rome was at peace for the first time in many decades. This image of tradition and peace was one that Augustus worked hard to maintain, though the idea that the whole Roman world was at peace at the time was an exaggeration. In 9 B.C., the Altar of Peace (Ara Pacis) was dedicated in Rome as an embodiment of the peace that he strived for throughout the empire. Its ornament included portraits of Augustus and his family, represented in ways that conveyed quasi-religious power and authority. Statues of the time, many of which were erected in Rome, represent Augustus as serious and focused, absorbed with his duties toward Rome. By now his enormous burial monument in the center of the city had been completed. It made an obvious statement about how important to Rome and its people he regarded himself.

The Emperor's Family Problems

In his later years, especially after 10 B.C., Augustus was much concerned with the question of what would happen to Rome after he died. Since his position and his entire career were anomalous for Rome, there existed no precedent. He had no legitimate sons. Augustus had hoped that either Gaius or Lucius, the sons of his daughter, Julia, might provide a successor. Augustus adopted them both. But the outlandish behavior of which Augustus accused his daughter in the year 2 B.C. almost destroyed his hopes that his grandsons would be considered suitable successors, as well as causing him acute embarrassment.

Although mentioned by many Roman writers, the episode is somewhat mysterious, because few details are provided. The facts appear to be as follows. In the latter part of the year 2, Augustus disowned and banished his only child, Julia, then thirty-seven years old, and publicly accused her of outrageous immoral behavior. She seems to have been charged with two main offenses—flagrantly enjoying the company of a series of lovers (while married to Tiberius, who was in self-imposed exile on the island of Rhodes at the time) and carousing repeatedly and openly in the Forum and other public places in the city, flaunting her contempt for her father's sense of decorum. Among the lovers who are named in the Roman texts are several men from prominent Roman families, and others are mentioned who were of no special note. Augustus sentenced one of these men, Iullus Antonius, to death; others he banished.

Julia's behavior particularly enraged Augustus, because he had worked hard to foster a return to what were perceived to be earlier traditions of moral uprightness in Roman society. He was a vehement advocate of what we would call family values. And his own daughter publicly and willfully violated the mores he was trying to reestablish.

Roman writers of the time and modern historians are divided in their interpretations of this episode. While it seems clear that Julia flagrantly challenged Augustus's program for moral regeneration for the city and behaved in the worst way possible for a daughter of the emperor, many observers believe that the harshness of the punishments Augustus meted out indicate that there was an important political aspect to the affair. Officially, Julia was banished, Iullus Antonius sentenced to death, and other of her lovers variously punished, because of their openly improper public behavior. But many commentators think that Julia and her associates were involved in a political conspiracy against Augustus and that his public outrage over the sexual indiscretions was a cover for his determination to eliminate the political threat. Several historians have suggested that Iullus Antonius, a member of a socially and politically significant family, may have had ambitions to achieve power in Rome.

Another important aspect to the story is that Augustus always treated Julia mainly as a pawn in his political machinations. When she was born, Augustus immediately divorced her mother, Scribonia, because Julia was not a male who could succeed him as emperor. Augustus forced her into a series of engagements—first at the age of two to Mark Antony's five-year-old son, who died as a child—and marriages to men with whom Augustus wanted to ally himself. One was his close associate Agrippa, with whom she traveled to and lived in the Roman east. When he died, Augustus compelled her to marry Tiberius, who was already married but whom Augustus forced to divorce his wife. Later Augustus's main interest in Julia seems to have been that she was the mother of his only blood relatives who could be heirs—Gaius and Lucius, sons of his friend Agrippa. As the historian A. H. M. Jones has put it, given the way Augustus treated his daughter throughout her young life, "it is not surprising that Julia went off the rails."

The punishment was harsh. Augustus banished Julia to Pandateria, a small island about thirty-five miles off the coast west of Naples. After five years there, she was moved to Rhegium, at the southern end of the Italian peninsula, where she died ten years later of starvation. Augustus further ordered that she not be buried in the mausoleum intended for his family at Rome.

Appointed as legates—advisers to military commanders—by Augustus in order that they might gain practical experience as young men, Gaius and Lucius began at an early age to serve the Roman cause. But Lucius died at Massilia, in southern Gaul, in A.D. 2, while traveling from Italy to Spain, and Gaius was wounded in Armenia in the east and died in A.D. 4. Thus Augustus's greatest hopes for an heir related by blood were gone. In desperation to have a successor whom he designated, Augustus adopted Tiberius, forty-five or forty-six years old at the time, immediately following Gaius's death. He was an experienced soldier who had proven his leadership abilities.

The Rhine Frontier and Augustus's German Policy

Augustus's greatest military challenge in the latter part of his life and the greatest military disaster of his career were to happen in the frontier regions on the Rhine. After Caesar's conquest of Gaul, completed in 51 B.C., written accounts about Gaul are relatively few (see chapter 7). Roman writers were occupied with the events of the civil wars that raged in Italy. As Augustus assumed near-absolute power in 27 B.C., he decided that the security and prosperity of Rome depended upon expanding the Empire's borders. Around 20 B.C., Gaul enters the Roman historical record again. In 20–19, Agrippa, Augustus's principal assistant for military affairs, was busy organizing the Roman road network and making other improvements in Gaul. According to written accounts, in the year 16, after capturing and executing a contingent of Roman soldiers east of the Rhine, a raiding party made up of members of the Sugambri, Usipetes, and Tencteri tribes crossed the river and attacked a Roman cavalry unit. Pursuing the fleeing troops, these invaders unexpectedly encountered the Fifth Legion, under the command of Marcus Lollius. The invaders defeated the legion and captured its eagle standard. This ignominious loss was among the events that made Augustus decide to go to Gaul to reorganize the Roman military there and to prepare Rhineland-based troops for campaigns into Germanic territory. A subsequent advance by Lollius and his forces, together with the impending arrival of Augustus, caused the invaders to recross the Rhine back to their homelands and to sue for peace with Rome.

Augustus remained in Gaul, the Rhineland, and Spain from 16 to 13 B.C., overseeing the reorganization of these territories and preparing for the upcoming campaigns. His adopted son, and later emperor, Tiberius accompanied him in Gaul to assist in these projects. At this time, Augustus established a mint at Lyon (Lugdunum), in Gaul, to provide a means of coining money to pay the troops, organized a census for collection of taxes in Gaul, and directed the establishment of military bases on the west bank of the Rhine (see chapter 5).

During these same years, the generals Tiberius and Drusus,

sons of his wife Livia, undertook the conquest of the Alpine tribes and the region between the Alps and the Danube, and they completed these conquests in 15 B.C. (see chapter 7). Three years later, the offensive against the Germanic peoples east of the middle and lower Rhine began in earnest, first led by Drusus, who pushed all the way eastward to the Elbe River and erected an altar there dedicated to his stepfather, the emperor. But this campaign, like others after it, while achieving successful passage of Roman troops through Germanic territory, did not conquer the peoples that inhabited it. Unlike the Gauls, whom Caesar conquered in 58–51 B.C., these Germanic tribal peoples had no major centers that they defended and that the Romans could make the focus of their attacks. This enemy was more mobile and flexible, and more difficult to defeat with Rome's military tactics. After Drusus's death, in 9 B.C., from injuries suffered when he fell from his horse while on campaign in Germany, his older brother, Tiberius, took over command of the Rhine forces.

Augustus's aims in these eastward campaigns are much debated today. The idea that Rome aspired to total conquest of the known world is discarded by many investigators. They argue that Augustus would have understood the impossibility of conquering and maintaining control over the vast lands, known to the Romans, east of the Rhine, to the north in Scandinavia, and to the northwest in Britain. More likely, Augustus maintained the political fiction of aiming at world domination, while realizing that such a goal was neither possible nor desirable.

After his return in 13 B.C., Augustus never again left Italy on a military mission. Between 6 B.C. and A.D. 4, Roman armies conducted a series of campaigns across the Rhine, many of them successful, but others marred by defeats and rebellions (see chapter 7). In A.D. 6, a time of many uprisings among the peoples Rome was trying to subdue east of the Rhine, the Roman armies, in concert with some Germanic military forces who were allied with them, had succeeded in isolating the eastern

Germanic leader Maroboduus in what was later Bohemia, now in the Czech Republic. These allied armies were ready to attack simultaneously from the Rhineland in the west and from the Danube region in the south. But then in A.D. 6 a rebellion broke out in Pannonia (roughly contiguous with modern Hungary and parts of Austria and Slovenia) and Dalmatia (roughly modern Croatia and Bosnia-Herzegovina). Tiberius had to quickly change plans to put down the uprising, and he was occupied there until A.D. 9 (see chapter 6). That year Tiberius, together with Drusus's son Germanicus, returned to Rome to great jubilation and honor after their successes in Pannonia. But before all of the celebrations were complete, news arrived that the Roman general Publius Quinctilius Varus, recently appointed Augustus's governor to manage affairs east of the Rhine, had led his troops into a catastrophic trap.

Augustus, already seventy-two years old, never recovered from the shock of this disaster. His daughter's acutely embarrassing misbehavior, the deaths of his grandsons, and the large and bloody uprising in Pannonia and Dalmatia had all caused him tremendous upset and disappointment, and the Teutoburg Forest defeat was the final blow to his spirit. In A.D. 13, Augustus named Tiberius his co-emperor, and effectively dropped out of active public life. In a statement that he had written to be read after his death, Augustus told Tiberius not to attempt any more conquests in the regions east of the Rhine. Augustus died August 19 in A.D. 14 in Nola, in Campania, 120 miles southeast of Rome.

5

VARUS AND THE FRONTIER

Rome's man in the Rhineland in A.D. 9 was Publius Quinctilius Varus. He had achieved an admirable record of service as governor and general elsewhere in the Empire, but in Germany he found himself totally unprepared for what was to come. Rome's blame for the catastrophe fell on his shoulders.

Opinions about Varus vary greatly among historians, ancient and modern, and the character of the man is important for understanding the background to the great battle. Velleius Paterculus, a soldier and historian and a contemporary of Varus who knew him personally, left a very unflattering profile. Tacitus, on the other hand, who wrote three generations after Varus's death, painted a much more positive picture of him. Different historians interpret the events leading up to the ambush and the course of the battle differently, depending upon which characterization of Varus they accept.

Varus and His Political Career

Publius Quinctilius Varus was born in 47 or 46 B.C. We know very little about the circumstances of his birth or childhood, or about either side of his family. The family of the Quinctilii apparently enjoyed patrician status, but had lost its prominence by the time Varus was born. Everything we know about him derives from his connections with Augustus and the political positions in which he served as the result of that relationship. He also benefited greatly from politically advantageous marriages. Although details of his personal life remain unknown, the available information about his career sheds light on the experience of a highly placed imperial functionary in the Roman elite.

The first fixed date in our knowledge of Varus's career is the year 13 B.C., when he served as consul with Claudius Nero, later known as Tiberius, the son of Augustus's wife Livia, who became Augustus's principal general, was adopted by the emperor in A.D. 2, and succeeded him as emperor. (Two consuls served as magistrates for both military and civil matters in Rome, and at this time they were appointed for annual terms by Augustus.) While serving as consul, Varus was married to a woman named Vipsania, who was a daughter of Augustus's close friend Agrippa, who had been governor of Gaul and occupied other important public positions. Later Varus married a woman named Claudia Pulchra, who was the daughter of a niece of Augustus's. One of Varus's sisters was married to another of Augustus's close friends, Lucius Nonius Asprenas. These marriage connections linked Varus closely to Augustus and provided him entry into the political elite of Rome. In his role as consul, Varus was able to ingratiate himself further with the emperor. When Augustus returned to Rome from the Rhineland and Gaul in 13 B.C., Varus and his co-consul organized the festivities in honor of the god Jupiter that celebrated the emperor's return. This opportunity gained Varus favor with Augustus and at the same time drew public attention to his active role in a big public spectacle. Besides the great celebrations, Augustus's return to Rome was marked by the dedication of the Altar of Peace, a highly visible and permanent monument to Augustus's successes in bringing peace to the provinces.

In the years 7–6 B.C., Varus served as proconsul of Africa, but we know very little about his experience there. Roman Africa at this time consisted of a narrow coastal territory between the Sahara Desert and the Mediterranean Sea, extending from modern eastern Algeria in the west to central Libya in the east. We are far better informed about his service as legate of Syria. Syria was an imperial province of Rome—its administration the direct responsibility of the emperor—and Augustus appointed Varus legate, his governing representative, in 6 B.C. In the accounts of his diplomatic, military, and political work there, we learn the most about what sort of a man Varus was and why Augustus chose him to become commander of the Roman army on the Rhine.

The position of governor in Syria was a difficult one, and Augustus's appointing of Varus to it indicates the emperor's great confidence in the man. Varus had to oversee several kingdoms, each with its own local ruler, as well as some major cities, within the province. Maintaining peace in this part of Rome's Empire required diplomatic ability as well as willingness to act with determination and ruthlessness when the situation required it. To the east, the Parthian Empire, controlling the lands between the Euphrates and Indus Rivers, provided a constant challenge to Roman peace in the region. This powerful state bordered the Roman Empire at the eastern end of Asia Minor, and the two rivals competed over the region of Armenia. Augustus's grandson and heir Gaius was to die in A.D. 4 as the result of a wound suffered in that theater of conflict, and a period of uneasy peace there followed.

Herod, king of Judea in the southwest part of the province, died in 4 B.C. (shortly after the birth of Jesus of Nazareth), and as governor Varus had to confront major uprisings that accompanied the succession struggle of this powerful Roman ally. According to the account of the Jewish historian Josephus, Varus controlled developments decisively and effectively. He brought one of the three legions stationed in Syria to Jerusalem to quell the disturbances there; later he sent the other two into the region to deal with uprisings elsewhere. Through skillful movements of different units of the army and application of force and threat of force at the right places, Varus succeeded in ending the disturbances in a relatively short time and bringing peace to the region. His actions in Syria indicate that he was able to command his military forces intelligently and to deal with complex regional crises effectively.

We do not know how long Varus remained in his position in Syria, nor do we know his successor. Probably in about 3 B.C. he ended his service there. From the time of his actions in quelling the rebellions in Palestine until his assumption of military command in Germany—a period of about a decade—we do not know where Varus was or what he did. In fact, between the years 6 B.C. and A.D. 5, we have comparatively little historical documentation about Rome as a whole.

Varus in Germany

In A.D. 7, Augustus appointed Varus his legate, or governor, for the Rhineland (see map 5). This position put him in charge of the legions stationed on the Rhine frontier and gave him responsibility for Rome's offensive policy in Germany east of the river. In the years A.D. 4 and 5, Tiberius had led large military campaigns east of the Rhine into Germany as far as the Elbe, where he linked with Roman naval ships that had advanced up the Elbe from the North Sea. He even spent the winter of A.D. 4–5 somewhere east of the Rhine, probably in one of the bases on the Lippe River (see below). By the end of the campaign season of A.D. 5, it appeared to Augustus and the rest of the Roman policymakers that Tiberius had successfully conquered Germany from the Rhine to the Elbe and that the land and its people were ready to be fully integrated into the provincial structure of the Roman Empire. A year later, the general Sentius Saturninus marched a large contingent of the army based at Mainz on the

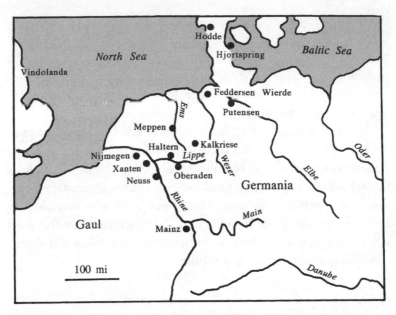

Map 5. Map showing places mentioned in chapters 5 and 6, associated with Roman policy in the Rhineland and with German activity east of the Rhine.

Rhine eastward toward what later became Bohemia. Their mission was to engage the forces of Maroboduus, leader of a tribal confederation that threatened the Roman frontier on the Danube. However, a rebellion in Pannonia and Dalmatia required a quick and massive military response (see chapter 6). The campaign against Maroboduus was called off, and Saturninus brought the legions back to their bases on the Rhine. This was the situation on the Rhine frontier when Varus assumed his new position.

Since Augustus and other Roman leaders considered the region between the Rhine and the Elbe conquered and ready for the introduction of provincial administration, Varus must have understood that his primary responsibility was creating Roman administrative structures, such as systems of census taking and taxation, among the tribal peoples of the region. From his experience in Syria, and from the outbreak of rebellion in Pannonia and Dalmatia, Varus was surely aware of the possibility of armed resistance to the expansion of Roman power and thus of the importance of his showing force during his administration. We have no information about Varus's actions during the year A.D. 8. It is quite possible, as Velleius Paterculus says, that Varus began to institute Augustus's policy of collecting taxes from the tribal groups, as if they were already part of Rome's provincial populations, but there is no clear evidence for this practice in Germany. If he did so, this action would certainly have added to the grievances that the Germanic tribes felt toward the Romans.

His presence in the Rhineland and in the territories east of the river between A.D. 7 and 9 is represented archaeologically by coins stamped with his name. A series of copper *as* coins (the Roman *as* denomination weighed about half an ounce) minted at Lyon, in Gaul, from 12 B.C. on bore a picture of Augustus on the obverse and of the Altar of Rome and Augustus, a monument erected in that political and religious center of Roman Gaul, on the reverse. These coins were intended to serve as payment to the soldiers. Many were subsequently stamped, not at the mint but at military bases, with countermarks that represented commanders of the legions. It was common practice for commanders to give monetary rewards to particular units of soldiers, sometimes to individuals, for outstanding service. The coins used for such gifts were often stamped with the donor's name to serve as a reminder of the source of the largesse. Such countermarked coins are found almost exclusively on military sites. Coins with the distinctive VAR countermark, for Varus, are common at military bases in the Rhineland, and they are well represented at the battle site of Kalkriese.

Varus's Character and the German Catastrophe

Modern as well as ancient opinion about Varus is mixed. As was mentioned earlier, Velleius Paterculus, who knew Varus personally, had only bad words for him, suggesting that he was incompetent as a military leader and that he enriched himself improperly during his governorship of Syria. According to Velleius, the Teutoburg Forest disaster was attributable to Varus's incompetence. Some modern historians, such as Theodor Mommsen, have largely accepted Velleius's assessment.

In contrast to Velleius, Tacitus says nothing uncomplimentary about Varus. The modern historians Walter John and Ronald Syme have held that Varus was a highly competent diplomat and military leader, who proved his consummate skills in Syria and was the ideal man for Augustus to place in the complex situation in Germany. John has suggested that Velleius's critical portrayal of Varus should be understood as the complaints of a cranky old soldier about an administrator who was given military command over the legions.

The judgment on Varus ultimately comes down to the question of who was to blame for the disaster in A.D. 9. Velleius and some other Roman writers placed the blame firmly on Varus, portraying him as lax, indolent, unable to see through the schemes of the crafty Arminius. Many modern commentators have accepted that representation and argued that Varus was the wrong person for the German post. But, as was noted above, this negative portrayal of Varus was by no means universal among Roman historians, and the accounts of his performance in Syria, in both the diplomatic and the military spheres, suggest that he was extremely competent. The lands east of the Rhine were of great concern to Augustus, and there is no reason to think that he would have placed a man in that position in whom he did not have the utmost confidence.

As I shall show in subsequent chapters, the reason for the Roman disaster in the Teutoburg Forest lay not in Varus's lack of ability or his misjudgment but instead in a much more pervasive misunderstanding of the political and social situation there on the part of Augustus and his advisers.

Life on the Roman Frontier

When, in A.D. 7, Varus became Augustus's governor and military commander of the Rhineland and the territories to the east, he arrived in a situation with well-established military bases and an ongoing military and diplomatic policy toward the Germanic peoples there. To understand what the army and the individual soldiers whom Varus commanded were like, we need to consider life on the Roman frontier at this time.

After Caesar's conquest of Gaul between 58 and 51 B.C., the Rhine River formed the eastern border of the new Roman territory. Caesar had made two forays across the Rhine, in 55 and 53, but had not conquered any territory there or defeated any tribal groups. In the decades following Caesar's conquest of Gaul, peoples east of the Rhine conducted numerous incursions westward across the river that were troublesome for the Roman authorities (see chapter 7). The defeat of a Roman legion under the command of Marcus Lollius in 16 B.C. (chapter 4) was a catalyst for a change in Roman policy—in particular, for a reorganization of Roman military forces in Gaul.

During his years in Gaul, Augustus directed the establishment of a provincial infrastructure that included a system for collecting taxes. At Lyon, he arranged the building of a central cult site for all of Gaul. It included an Altar of Rome and Augustus, to honor both the center of the Empire and himself as first citizen. He also reorganized the deployment of the legions, moving them from the interior of Gaul to the frontier along the banks of the Rhine. He oversaw the construction of a series of new military bases, at what are today Nijmegen, Xanten, Moers-Asberg, Neuss, Mainz, and perhaps Bonn. The chief purpose of these bases was to stop incursions into the Roman territory by groups from across the Rhine, but the troops could also be called upon to deal with uprisings within the province, as they had to be in

12 B.C. when disturbances broke out over taxation. At the same time, these frontier bases provided ideal locations from which to launch campaigns into the regions east of the Rhine. Those at Xanten and Mainz, in particular, were situated just across the Rhine from the confluences of rivers—the Lippe and the Main—that provided water access into the interior of Germanic territory. A naval fleet was built for moving supplies and troops along the Rhine and up those slow, westward-flowing rivers. In 12 B.C., massive military campaigns began, under the command of Augustus's adopted son Drusus, against the Germanic tribes east of the Rhine. The troops set out from the bases at Xanten and Mainz and moved eastward up the valleys of the Lippe and Main Rivers, in a pincer strategy that was intended to converge on the powerful tribes in the German interior.

The details of this summer campaign, and its relation to later events, will be explored in chapter 7. Our subject here is life in the military bases on the Rhine frontier and at the forward bases established across the Rhine along the routes of penetration into the Germanic lands. What was the military experience for the soldiers who followed Varus into the German forests and perished at the hands of Arminius and his warriors?

The Rhine Bases

When first established by Augustus's orders between 15 and 12 B.C. in preparation for the new offensives into Germanic territory, the bases along the Rhine were temporary affairs, without the solid stone architecture that we associate with Roman fortresses. The familiar image of a Roman military base—from movies, drawings in books and magazines, and reconstructions in museums and on archaeological sites—is of a huge defensive wall of cut stone blocks enclosing stone-and-mortar barracks, officers' quarters, administration buildings, workshops, and a hospital, all solidly built on a regular plan. But these sturdy and precisely organized forts were constructed only in a later phase of Roman activity in the Rhine and Danube provinces, after the middle of the first century A.D. The early camps featured exterior V-shaped double ditches on the outside, and walls built of two rows of vertical wooden planks set about nine feet apart, with the earth from the ditches filling the space between them. Instead of stone, barracks, officers' residences, workshops, and the hospital were all made of wood. Gates at the entrances and guard towers were also built of timber.

Mainz (Mogontiacum)

In about 13 B.C., the Roman forces established a base to accommodate two legions at Mainz. The base was situated on a plateau about a hundred feet above the Rhine; this afforded a broad view in all directions. The fortification consisting of a double ditch and a wall of wood and earth enclosed roughly ninety acres. Excavations have yielded pits and foundation ditches, probably for barracks. Historical sources inform us that the First and Fifth Legions were stationed at Mainz, under the command of Lucius Asprenas.

In addition to abundant subsurface structures and large quantities of pottery, tools, weapons, and other materials from the military base at Mainz, a unique monument associated with the Roman campaigns across the Rhine still stands on the site. After the general Drusus died, as the result of a fall from his horse during his return from the summer campaign in Germany in 9 B.C., his troops brought his body to the base at Mainz, where the soldiers performed ceremonies in his honor. His brother Tiberius later accompanied the body to Pavia, in northern Italy, and Augustus led the funeral procession from Pavia to Rome. At the base in Mainz, the soldiers erected a monument to their leader, and the enormous stone structure, on a promontory overlooking the Rhine, still stands, sixty-four feet high. This cylindrical tower was visible throughout the surrounding landscape, from both sides of the Rhine, and served to remind the troops of their highly regarded leader, who had given his life in the pursuit of the new province east of the Rhine.

Xanten (Vetera), Varus's Rhineland Base

The fortress at Xanten was the base from which Varus operated when he departed on his fateful campaign of A.D. 9. The legionary camp of Vetera was founded in 13 or 12 B.C., shortly before Drusus's campaign in the summer of that year. Located on the southern slope of the Fürstenberg, just south of the modern city of Xanten, on the west bank of the Rhine, it provided a broad view over the flat surrounding landscape. Directly across the Rhine was the mouth of the Lippe River (the confluence is now farther south), and General Drusus began his summer offensive of 12 B.C. by heading up the Lippe valley. From Xanten's founding, five successive legionary bases have been identified through excavation on the site. Current archaeological evidence from the first fort at Xanten is sparse, but much of the area remains to be investigated. A ditch, two kilns in which pottery was fired, a wall built of earth and wood, and many pit structures make up the clearest evidence for this earliest phase of the fort.

We do not know for certain which legions were stationed at Xanten between its founding and A.D. 9. The discovery on the site of the gravestone of Marcus Caelius, a centurion of the Eighteenth Legion who was killed in the Battle of the Teutoburg Forest (see illustration 14)—the only clear archaeological evidence, before the discoveries since 1987 at Kalkriese, that the battle ever took place—makes it very likely that the Eighteenth Legion was stationed here (see below). That legion was annihilated with Varus in A.D. 9, and it was never reconstituted.

Haltern—A Roman Outpost among the Germans

As Mainz and Xanten are examples of early bases on the Rhine, Haltern is a well-studied advance fort in Germany east of the Rhine. It is on the Lippe River, eleven miles upstream from where it flows into the Rhine opposite Xanten. As is already apparent with the founding of Xanten in 13 or 12 B.C., Drusus selected the Lippe as an ideal route eastward into the heart of Germany, and the Romans established a series of fortresses along the river, five of which have been identified through archaeological research, to serve as bases for the advances toward the Elbe. We do not know the Roman names for these places, since they are not mentioned in any surviving texts. They are known today exclusively by the local German place-names—from west to east, Holsterhausen, Haltern, Beckinghausen, Oberaden, and Anreppen. As a small, slow-flowing river without falls or rapids, the Lippe was ideal as a water route for moving men and supplies inland from the Rhine. Shipping on the Lippe saved great amounts of time and energy, compared with land marches and hauling of goods by pack animal and wagon. In addition to providing the resources needed by the troops as they sought to bring the Germanic territories under control, the Roman foundation at Haltern was probably also intended to form an administrative base for the establishment of the infrastructure for the new province, once the lands and peoples had been fully conquered and integrated. Varus probably spent time with his legions at Haltern, which may have been their base during the final winter before the fateful summer of A.D. 9.

Archaeologists have identified six Roman sites at Haltern (see illustration 15). Three of these—the main base, the naval harbor, and the port—are particularly important for this account. The complex was founded about 5 B.C. and was abandoned—hastily—in A.D. 9. The archaeological evidence from this base allows us to reconstruct what life was like for a soldier stationed here during the legions's forays eastward toward the Elbe. The main base at Haltern covered forty-seven acres and was surrounded by a defensive system of two ditches and a wall built of timber and earth (illustration 16). Four gates led into the interior of the fortress. A Roman soldier stationed here would have felt a certain measure of protection from the standard military bank-and-ditch defense, with guards posted along the walls, even though he knew he was in German, not Roman, territory.

Inside the defensive perimeter was a small city with all of the administrative, economic, and residential functions that a legion of some five thousand men, together with support staff, required. The main street in the fortress ran between the east and west gates. The principal cross street led to the headquarters at the center of the base, which served as the command and administration building, the pay office, and the site of the sanctuary in which the legion's standards were kept. The fort commander's office and residence were next to the headquarters, as were the houses of other high-ranking officers. Barracks for the soldiers, designed to accommodate as many men as possible rather than to provide comfort, were arranged along the outside edge of the fort. Other important buildings on the base were the hospital and the blacksmith's shop, where weapons and tools were made and repaired. Just outside the fort's walls were kilns for firing pottery for everyday cooking and serving of food, finer decorative ceramics, and oil lamps.

The size of the base at Haltern and the composition of its interior suggest that it was not a typical legionary base, but rather one intended for special administrative purposes beyond those of the unit stationed there. The number of houses designed for officers is unusually high, perhaps because Haltern was being developed to serve as an administrative center.

Not everything that archaeologists have found at Haltern conforms to the picture of a smoothly running army base. In one of the pits in which potters had worked their clay were skeletons of at least twenty-four men. Other signs of disruption are buried hoards. One pit thirteen feet in diameter and thirteen feet deep contained thousands of iron arrowheads, together with iron axes and wagon tires, fragments of bronze, and glass beads. Another pit contained a helmet, an iron lance, two bronze pails, and iron tools. A hoard of coins included 185 silver denarii and one aureus—an amount equivalent to the annual salary of a legionary soldier. The latest coin in the hoard, represented by 71 specimens, is a denarius with images of Augustus's grandsons Gaius and Lucius, minted between 2 B.C. and A.D. 4. The next denarius type minted by Rome appeared in A.D. 13. Since none of these later coins is represented in the hoard, the hoard was most likely buried between 2 B.C. and A.D. 13, probably by a soldier who was never able to retrieve it.

Nearly 3,000 Roman coins have been recovered at Haltern, and coins are common finds at all of the Rhineland bases. A recent compilation of the Haltern coins counted 2,561 copper, 293 silver, and 2 gold coins. Soldiers carried money with them in leather, cloth, or bronze purses, both at their bases and on campaigns. They used their money for a variety of purposes. They bought things from their comrades, sometimes paid others to carry out camp duties assigned to them, and shopped in the native settlements around the bases. A favorite way of passing leisure time was in gambling. In the Roman world at this time, gambling at games of luck such as dice and board games was enjoyed by many people, including the emperor Augustus. The city of Rome had rules against gambling in public except during the festival of Saturnalia, in mid-December, an indication of how popular and distracting these games must have been. At Roman military bases, where soldiers presumably could engage in such games whenever they were not on duty, archaeological finds of dice carved from bone and of gaming pieces—slightly smaller than modern checkers and made of stone or animal bone—are common. The soldiers probably played for low stakes for amusement, rather than trying to win a lot of money from their fellows.

Southeast of the main base at Haltern and situated directly on the Lippe River was a naval station. A fortification consisting of double ditches, each pointed at the bottom, and a wood-and-earth wall, like those at the main base on the hill, enclosed it on three sides, and the fourth side was open to the water. Foundations of eight slips for boats, measuring 94 by 20 feet, show that large ships were based here, kept inside the shelters in bad weather, perhaps through the winter months.

Also on the Lippe, due south of the main base, was a harbor town, established by the Roman army but inhabited largely by people from the area. Here supplies were unloaded for the whole military complex at Haltern, and a variety of port functions were provided. Local crafts workers, who lived in nearby villages, produced goods wanted by the soldiers, such as ornaments for their uniforms, belts, sandals, and tools. Farmers sold meat, fruit, vegetables, and beer, offering the troops diversions from their standard diet. Innkeepers sold prepared meals, and prostitutes offered their services. Probably some unofficial families of the soldiers lived in the harbor town as well. For these varied reasons, some of the soldiers surely spent much of their leisure time in this part of the Haltern complex.

Soldiers were not allowed to marry, but many became involved in relationships with local women, and some had families. The families were not permitted to live in the military bases (officers, however, were allowed to have their families on the bases), but they often lived in the towns nearby. Many soldiers, when they completed their terms of service, settled down near the base where they had been stationed, using their veterans' pensions to purchase land and to build or buy a house. Near military bases that lasted longer than Haltern, such as those on the west bank of the Rhine at Xanten, Cologne, and Mainz, substantial settlements often developed. Their populations included native people who moved to the site to earn money by producing goods for the soldiers; families begun by soldiers on active duty; veterans and their families; and all manner of merchants, entertainers, and others who wished to capitalize on the presence of a large number of well-paid men eager for new goods and entertainment. As these communities grew in size, many took on the character of Mediterranean towns, with stone architecture, paved streets, aqueducts to deliver fresh water and underground drains to carry away waste, and the typical Roman infrastructure of temples, public baths, and arenas. Although the predominant language heard on the street would have been the local version of Germanic or Celtic, otherwise such a town looked like a very small version of Rome. Similar urban bustle, marketing of foodstuffs and craft products, aromas of cooking foods, and manufacture of pottery, tools, textiles and other materials defined the urban character. Soldiers from distant parts of the Empire and itinerant merchants contributed to the cosmopolitan aspect of the community.

The Legions at Xanten, at Haltern, and in the Great Battle

The organization of the Roman army changed over time, and it is important that we consider its structure immediately before the fateful battle. Augustus was the first Roman ruler to form a professional standing army loyal to the Roman state. At the time of the reorganization of the military in Gaul and the Rhineland, there were twenty-eight legions, each designated by a number and commanded by a legate, a man of senatorial rank. A legion consisted of about 5,000 men, but the size varied somewhat. It was divided into a number of smaller units. Ten cohorts were each made up of about 480 soldiers, and each cohort was further broken down into six centuries of about 80 men, commanded by a centurion. The smallest unit was the *contubernium*, consisting of

8 men, who shared a tent on campaign and a room in the barracks on the bases.

In addition to these 4,800 infantry soldiers, the legion had a
cavalry force of some 120 men and horses, together with crafts-
men, medical specialists, and officers. The legionary legate, or
commander, was assisted by a tribune of high rank, a camp prefect, and five tribunes of lesser rank. Each legion had one soldier
whose job was to carry the imperial eagle of that legion, and
each century had a soldier who carried that century's standards.

Life in the Bases

When Roman troops built a new base, as they did at Xanten in
13 or 12 B.C. and at Haltern around 5 B.C., they first laid out the
main cross streets and sites of the four gates, using surveying
instruments, including lead plumb bobs. Next, they dug the
outer ditches, using iron-headed picks and shovels, and constructed the wood-and-earth wall. For the main base at Haltern,
some 12,500 oak trees were felled for the wood, by means of
sturdy iron axes. For temporary camps, just the ditches and an
earth wall were constructed, as Julius Caesar describes in his
commentary on his campaigns in Gaul.

The principal food in the soldiers' diet was grain, mainly
wheat, often eaten in the form of baked bread or a stew of grain,
vegetables, and salted meat. Grain was stored in a base granary
and distributed to individual soldiers. Meat was consumed in
small amounts, relative to the typical modern diet in America and
Western Europe. Spices, especially pepper, added zest to food, as
did the favorite Roman fish sauce, *garum*. All soldiers had some
wine, which they diluted with water, but officers had more and
better wine. Unlike modern military bases, the Roman bases had
no mess hall. Soldiers cooked their own food, often with the
seven other members of their *contubernium*. Grindstones for

1. Woodcut by Hans Brosamer, 1543, showing
Arminius holding the head of Varus. From Burkart
Waldis, *Ursprung und Herkumen der zwölf ersten König
und Fürsten Deutscher Nation* (Nuremberg).

2. Copper engraving by Sandrart, 1689,
showing Arminius in battle armor and
holding tankard. From Daniel Casper
Lohenstein, *Grossmüthiger Feldherr
Arminius* (Leipzig).

3. Copper
statue of Arminius
near Detmold,
in northern
Germany.

4. The three lead slingstones that provided the first direct evidence that a battle involving Roman troops took place at Kalkriese. The slingstone at lower left is about 1.5 inches long.

5. Iron weapons recovered from the battlefield: two cat-apult bolt points, a lance shoe (end opposite point, for sticking in the ground), three lance heads, and a fragmentary dagger. Largest point is about 8 inches long.

6. RIGHT. Iron point of a javelin (*pilum*) recovered from the battlefield. Length 7 inches.

7. BELOW RIGHT. Iron pick-ax (*dolabra*), Roman tool with an ax blade at one end and a broad pick at the other, recovered from the battlefield. This tool was used for clearing underbrush and digging ditches around temporary military camps. Length 21 inches.

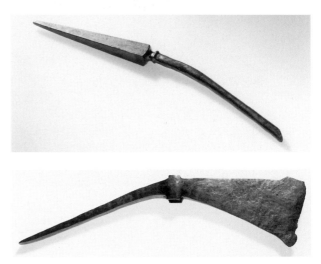

8. Four lead plumb bobs, used by Roman military engineers for laying out camps. The bottom object is about 0.7 inches long.

9. Two Roman surgical instruments. The top object is a handle from a surgical knife. Its ends contain silver inlay. The bottom object is a probe. Military doctors used such implements to tend the wounded soldiers. Length of probe about 6 inches.

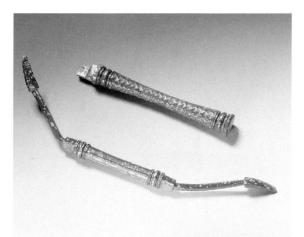

10. Characteristic Roman women's bronze jewelry, a pin and two fragmentary brooches. These are among the objects found on the battlefield that suggest women were present among the Roman troops and were killed in the battle along with the legionaries. The pin is about 5 inches long.

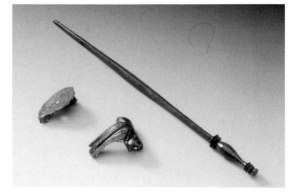

11. Skeleton of a
mule discovered on
the battlefield.

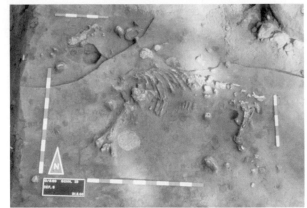

12. Marble statue
of Cleopatra. Height
about 24 inches.

13. The Gemma Augustea, a cut stone representation
showing Augustus seated as Jupiter on a throne, next
to the spirit of Rome. On the left, the victorious
general Tiberius steps from a chariot. On the
bottom, Roman soldiers raise a trophy of captured
enemy weapons above the defeated and bound
captives. Width 9 inches.

14. Gravestone of Marcus Caelius, a
centurion of the Eighteenth Legion
who was killed in the Battle of the
Teutoburg Forest. Height 54 inches.

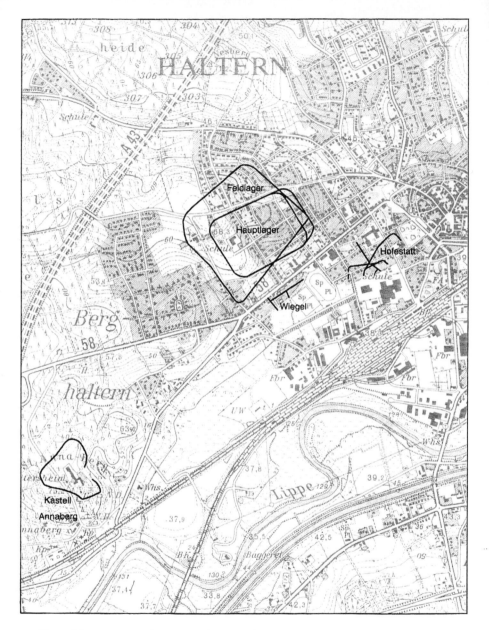

15. Plan of the Roman military complex at Haltern. Hauptlager, main base. Hofestatt, the naval station (originally directly on the Lippe River, the course of which has since been changed). Wiegel, the port (also originally on the Lippe).

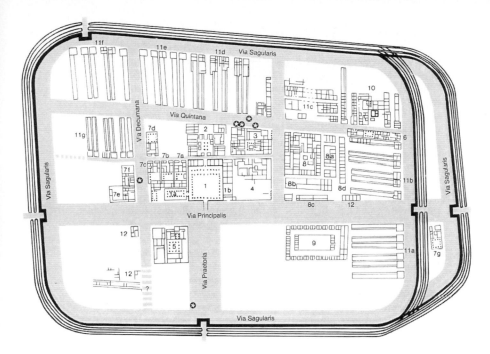

16. Plan of the main Roman military base at Haltern, the best-documented base of Augustan times. The plan shows the double ditches on the outside, the wall inside of them, the principal streets, and the complex of buildings that have been excavated: 1, headquarters; 2, 3, 7, residences of the base commander and of high officers; 8, workshops; and 9, hospital.

17. Iron catapult bolt point with the stamp LEG XIX, indicating the Nineteenth Legion. Found at Döttenbichl, near Oberammergau in southern Bavaria. Length 2 inches.

18. Reconstruction drawing of the Iron Age village of Hodde, in Denmark.

20. Iron nails from Roman military sandals recovered from the battle site at Kalkriese.

21. Representation of the triumph of Tiberius in 8 or 7 B.C., on the silver cup from Boscoreale, in Italy. The scene shows Tiberius riding in a horse-drawn chariot through the streets of Rome, being crowned with the laurel wreath of victory. Height about 4 inches.

19. OPPOSITE. Objects from Grave 150 at Putensen. They include an iron sword, spearheads, and a shield boss, six spurs, numerous brooches, two Roman bronze casseroles, and a large bronze-and-iron cauldron.

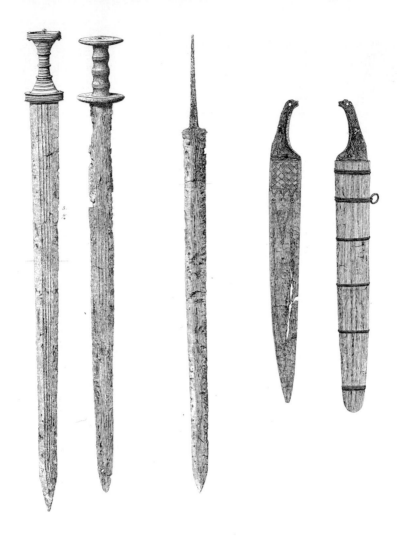

22. Iron swords from Nydam (three on left) and Vimose (without and with scabbard), Denmark. The three from Nydam are all two-edged; that from Vimose is one-edged. The sword on the far left has a wooden handle ornamented with silver bands, length 36 inches. The next has a bone handle, length 34 inches. The sword in the middle is missing its handle, length 34 inches. The sword from Vimose is 23 inches long. From C. Engelhardt, *Nydam Mosefund* (Copenhagen, 1865), pl. 6, 3. 4, pl. 7, 15, and *Vimose Mosefundet* (Copenhagen, 1869), pl. 7, 26. 27.

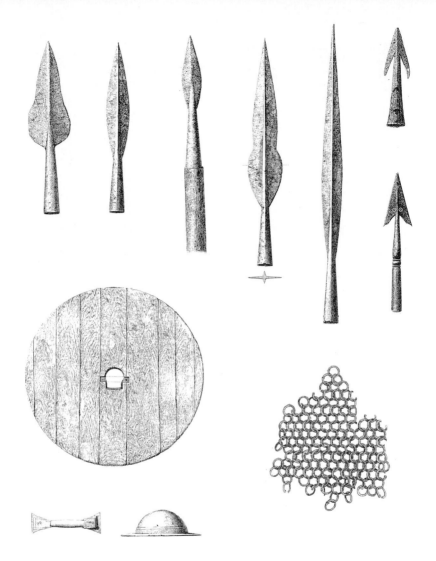

23. Iron spearheads from Nydam and Vimose, shield and fittings from Thorsberg in
Germany, and chain mail from Vimose. The spearheads show the range of sizes and
shapes represented. All are drawn to the same scale, and the longest is 17 inches
long. The third from the left was found complete with its wooden shaft. It was a
javelin, with a total length of about 10 feet. The wooden shield is 40 inches in
diameter. Below the shield are a wooden shield handle, covered with sheet bronze,
and a bronze shield boss (attached to the front of the shield to cover the handle).
The chain mail fragment is about 3 by 2.25 inches in size. From Engelhardt, *Thorsb-*
jerg Mosefund (Copenhagen, 1863), pl. 8, 1. 6. 11a, *Nydam Mosefund* (Copenhagen,
1865), pl. 10, 5. 9. 10. 12. 19, and *Vimose Mosefundet* (Copenhagen, 1869), pl. 4, 2.

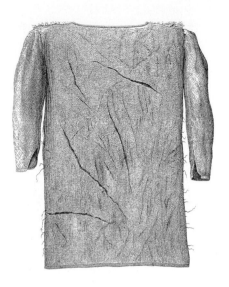

24. Woolen tunic from Thorsberg.
From Engelhardt, *Thorsbjerg Mosefund*
(Copenhagen, 1863), pl. 1, 1.

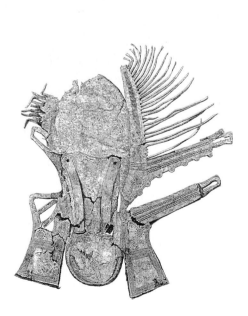

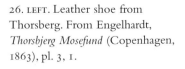

25. ABOVE. Woolen pants from
Thorsberg. From Engelhardt,
Thorsbjerg Mosefund (Copenhagen,
1863), pl. 2, 1.

26. LEFT. Leather shoe from
Thorsberg. From Engelhardt,
Thorsbjerg Mosefund (Copenhagen,
1863), pl. 3, 1.

27. Roman silver denarius coin, minted in 48 or 47 B.C., shortly after Julius Caesar's conquest of Gaul. It shows a captive enemy and a trophy of weapons.

28. Large bronze bell found stuffed with straw, with a mule skeleton, on the battle site. Length 6.5 inches.

29. Iron face mask, with remains of original silver coating still apparent around edges, found near the wall on the battle site. Height 6.7 inches.

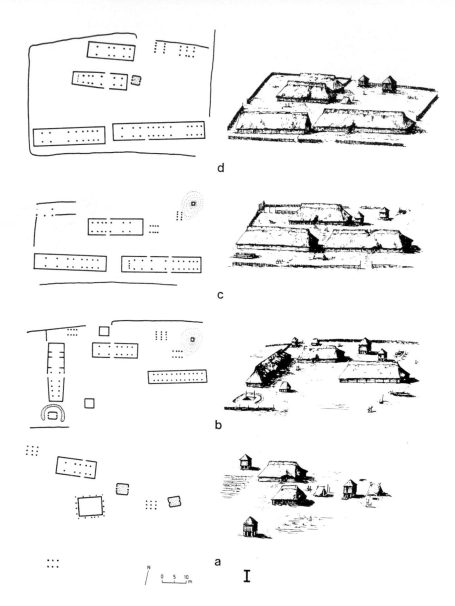

30. Plans (left) and reconstruction drawings (right) showing the development of the settlement at Flögeln, in northern Germany: *a*, farm as the earliest settlement; *b*, farm complex in the second phase, showing larger buildings and enclosing fences, aspects of a more complex and specialized economy; *c* and *d*, later phases of development, in the late first and second centuries A.D.

preparing grain, ceramic cooking pots, jugs, plates, knives, and spoons were the equipment for food preparation and consumption, and examples of all of these items have been recovered by archaeologists on Roman bases. Officers used finer ceramics and more spices and generally consumed better foods than did the soldiers. On campaign, soldiers carried their rations in their packs, usually their personal supply for three days. A bronze-handled pot called a casserole was the all-purpose cooking vessel when they were on the march.

Food, equipment, and other goods were supplied to Roman bases largely by boat, except for what the soldiers could acquire from local people who lived and farmed around their bases. Before the invention of motorized vehicles and the building of railroads and highways, water transport was the most practical way of moving freight. The Rhine and the Lippe Rivers provided easy access by boat to the bases such as Mainz, Xanten, and Haltern. Archaeologists have found and studied many Roman boats from the Rhine and know a great deal about shipping technology. At the site of the port just south of the base at Haltern, great quantities of grain and sherds of amphoras reflect goods that were spilled and broken in the process of transfer from ships on the Lippe to storage facilities at the base. Remains of some 850 amphoras have been found so far at Haltern, about half of them of the type for transporting fish sauce and a quarter each for wine and olive oil. Wine was probably shipped largely in wooden barrels, which have not survived as often as ceramic amphoras have.

The quantities of food required by the Roman troops were enormous. A legion consumed over two thousand tons of wheat per year; the horses of a cavalry unit, over six hundred tons of barley. When a base relied largely on the surrounding countryside to produce its food, this demand could put a tremendous strain on the local farmers. But at the same time it offered a highly profitable cash resource for communities that had been accustomed to dealing mostly in barter trade. When grain, meat,

and other supplies were not available locally, the logistical problems of bringing the goods in from outside, by boat up the Rhine and Lippe, were formidable.

At the time that Haltern was in use, the legionary soldier was paid 225 silver denarii a year for his service, usually in three installments of 75 denarii each. To put this amount into context, one denarius was equal to sixteen asses, the copper coins in common use. Twelve copper coins would purchase a week's ration of grain. A liter of cheap wine cost one as; a liter of the best wine, four. A centurion earned up to fifteen times as much as a legionary soldier, and the commander of the first cohort in each legion, up to sixty times as much. Sometimes pay was augmented by gifts from the emperor or local commander, or by shares in goods captured from defeated enemies. The soldiers had to pay for their own food and clothing and for the upkeep of their weapons; amounts to cover these expenses were usually deducted from their salary before they received the cash, leaving them about half of their official salary, which they received in coin. They often had money left to spend at the shops and inns in the town outside the base. They liked to buy trinkets of various kinds, purchase wine of better quality than that available on the base, entertain women, and gamble at the games of luck that they enjoyed so much in their off-duty time. After twenty or twenty-five years of service, a retiring veteran received a pension of 3,000 denarii—the equivalent of thirteen years' pay.

What Was Life Like for the Soldiers?

Despite the great emphasis in the study of the Roman military on fighting and marching on campaign, most of the time most of the soldiers, like their modern counterparts, were not fighting. Only during the summer months did the soldiers based on the Rhine at Mainz and Xanten, and those on the Lippe at Haltern

leave the bases to go on campaigns eastward into Germany. Even then, they spent most of their time in marching, setting up temporary camps, and generally "showing the flag"—in this case, the Roman standards.

Drills were a regular, probably daily, occurrence. Maneuvers were carried out periodically, to keep the soldiers in shape and practiced at cutting roads, building bridges, and constructing camps. The men had to clean and polish their weapons to pass the frequent inspections. Soldiers did a lot of building and repair work on the bases and were responsible for cutting wood in the forests for construction and for fires, for procuring foodstuffs through purchase and trade in the countryside around the bases, and for other everyday tasks. Many worked at the crafts that were required to keep the legions supplied with weapons, tools, clothing, and cooking supplies. Roman bases were outfitted with all of the essential facilities that the legions required. A blacksmith shop made and repaired weapons and tools. A pottery workshop produced the containers needed for preparing and serving food. Every base had a hospital, complete with medical personnel, surgical instruments, and medicinal chemicals and plants to treat diseases and wounds.

The length of time that a unit was stationed at a particular base varied greatly, depending upon where the emperor and his generals decided that troops were needed. Soldiers sometimes felt they had to work too hard at their daily tasks on the bases. Describing circumstances on the Rhine in A.D. 14, Tacitus writes, "They complained about the hardness of the work and specifically about building ramparts, digging ditches, foraging, collecting timber and firewood, and all the other camp tasks that are either necessary or invented to keep men busy."

Like most soldiers, legionaries stationed at the bases in the Rhineland surely met and courted local women in their spare time, though we do not have much specific information about these relationships. But the informal meeting of soldiers and natives was an important vehicle for the transmission of cultural knowledge. Soldiers got to know the people who lived around their bases, and the locals became familiar with some of the troops stationed in their vicinity. Through dealings with local women, friendships with farmers, and transactions with vendors of food, wine, and craft products, soldiers learned about the peoples on whose lands they were stationed and thus formed relationships very different from the official ones between Rome and its provinces. As a result, many soldiers probably developed attitudes toward these peoples that differed from the stereotypical views expressed in the writings of the authors back in Rome.

The physical remains of architecture, pottery, tools, and food debris can provide us with a good idea about the material aspects of the legionaries' lives. From a base distant in time and space from Mainz, Xanten, and Haltern, we can learn also about the thoughts of some of the people at the bases on the imperial frontier. At the Roman site of Vindolanda, near Hadrian's Wall in northern Britain, unusual conditions of preservation have led to the survival of hundreds of letters written with ink on thin pieces of wood between A.D. 90 and 120. They offer direct insight into the personal lives of some of those stationed in the frontier bases. For example, one is a note about an individual's clothing supplies—"I have sent you . . . pairs of socks from Sattua two pairs of sandals and two pairs of underpants." Another is a birthday party invitation, written to the wife of the base commander— "On the third day before the Ides of September, sister, for the day of the celebration of my birthday, I give you a warm invitation to make sure that you come to us, to make the day more enjoyable for me by your arrival." Reading such personal messages makes us realize that, in many respects, the Roman soldiers and their families were not very different from us.

Xanten, Haltern, and the Doomed Legions

It is almost certain that many of the Roman legionaries who died in the great battle in the Teutoburg Forest lived in the bases at Xanten and Haltern shortly before their fateful march eastward. The legions that were annihilated in that event, the Seventeenth, Eighteenth, and Nineteenth, were raised by Octavian sometime between 41 and 30 B.C. and were stationed on the Rhine.

We know very little about the Seventeenth Legion. For the Eighteenth, we have more information. The tombstone of the centurion Marcus Caelius (illustration 14), who was killed in the Battle of the Teutoburg Forest, is an important piece of archaeological evidence for the Eighteenth Legion. The stone was found at Xanten, and that is probably where he was stationed. This gravestone offers the only portrait that we possess of an individual who fought in that battle. (Though coins were minted in North Africa during Varus's service as proconsul there, the head on the obverse is thought not to be a true portrait of Varus.) The tombstone, which is fifty-four inches high, marked a cenotaph—a grave that contained no body—because his body was not recovered from the battlefield. Like modern gravestones, it has an inscription that tells us much about the deceased individual and his role in the Roman army.

Marcus Caelius was born in Bologna, Italy, and was a centurion of the top rank in the Eighteenth Legion. He was fifty-three and a half years old when he died in the battle, serving with Varus. The two heads on either side are those of slaves whom he freed, named Marcus Caelius Privatus and Marcus Caelius Thiaminus. The sculpture shows the fallen centurion framed by a small temple, a typical feature in Roman cemeteries. He wears body armor decorated with five medallions, and he is equipped with a variety of symbols of rank and honor. In his right hand, he holds the staff that marks his rank as centurion. On each wrist, he wears a bracelet. On his head is a crown of oak leaves—an award given for saving the life of another Roman citizen—and on each shoulder an ornamental ring with buffer ends. This representation shows how he looked when dressed for ceremonial occasions, such as military parades and victory celebrations.

The archaeological indicators of the Nineteenth Legion are more abundant and more varied, and they all attest to this legion's service on the frontier in Germany. Recent excavations at Döttenbichl, near Oberammergau in southern Bavaria, have recovered, together with other Roman weapons, three iron catapult bolt points with the legend LEG XIX (see illustration 17; see also chapter 7). Roman historical sources tell us that in 15 B.C. the generals Tiberius and Drusus led campaigns to conquer the lands between the Alps and the Danube, and this bolt and the associated objects are consistent with this date. These objects indicate that the Nineteenth Legion participated in this conquest of what is today southern Bavaria, probably under the command of Drusus.

A small bronze tag bearing the number XIX was recovered in excavations at the Roman frontier base at Dangstetten, on the upper Rhine in southwest Germany, a fortress that served as a launching point for the conquest and pacification of the peoples in southern Germany. This tag indicates that at least part of the Nineteenth Legion was stationed there at some time between 15 and 7 B.C. It is thought that when Augustus and his advisers judged that the region had been successfully subdued, he ordered the Nineteenth Legion to Cologne, on the lower Rhine.

In excavations at Haltern in 1964, a lead ingot weighing about 140 pounds was found. On one side of the rectangular bar, a chiseled legend reads CCIII L XIX. CCIII indicates the weight—203 Roman pounds—and L XIX names the Nineteenth Legion. Lead was used for many purposes on Roman bases, and several other ingots have been recovered at Haltern. This ingot, marked as a possession of the Nineteenth Legion, is the first archaeological discovery between the Rhine and Elbe Rivers that names one of the legions that were annihilated in the battle in the Teutoburg Forest.

In his account of the visit by the general Germanicus and his troops to the battle site six years after the event (see chapter 11), Tacitus informs us that the eagle of the Nineteenth Legion had been captured by the enemy troops in their defeat of Varus.

The End of Haltern

The Roman base at Haltern, eleven miles into Germanic territory from the Rhine, was abandoned hurriedly in A.D. 9. No written sources mention the base, and we are completely dependent upon the archaeological evidence. The hoards of weapons, tools, and coins found at Haltern show that the occupants buried items they did not want to fall into enemy hands—weapons of war and treasure. Another kind of evidence also indicates hurried departure. Among the items of pottery recovered through excavation on the site, the proportion of complete ceramic vessels is exceptionally high. Most of the pottery that we find on settlement sites is in the form of fragmentary sherds. Plates, bowls, and cups break through everyday use, and the fragments become trodden into the ground where they fall, or where people toss them. Under ordinary conditions, when people leave a place, they take usable goods with them. Legions departing from Haltern under peaceful conditions would have taken their pottery, especially the ornate and popular fine ware known as terra sigillata. The unusually high proportion of terra sigillata vessels found intact at Haltern indicates that the troops did not depart under planned, peaceful circumstances. The twenty-four skeletons in the kiln pit suggest that the community came to a violent end.

The date of Haltern's end can be fixed through the coins. Among the large and varied assemblage of coins recovered on the site, many belong to the years before A.D. 9, but none after that year. We will see a similar pattern among the coins found at Kalkriese, where the legions based at Haltern met their end. When they learned of the disaster at Kalkriese, the small garrison left behind at Haltern apparently fled in terror westward, back to the safety of the Rhine bases. All of the other short-lived bases on the Lippe River—Anreppen, Oberaden, and Holsterhausen—were also abandoned out of fear that Arminius was about to sweep through the valley, slaughtering Roman soldiers there as he had at Kalkriese, just sixty miles to the northeast.

6

ARMINIUS: THE NATIVE HERO

Roman historical sources inform us that Arminius, a prince in the Cherusci tribe of Germans who lived in what is today northern Germany, had served with the Roman army, in command of auxiliary forces, probably composed of members of his tribe. We do not know precisely where he served, but it is likely that he gained firsthand experience in Roman military tactics while helping Tiberius suppress the great rebellion that broke out in Pannonia in A.D. 6.

In the region of Pannonia and Dalmatia, there were numerous warlike tribal peoples at this time. Although Augustus thought that they had been brought under control by Tiberius around 10 B.C., they nonetheless displayed restlessness under Roman domination. In A.D. 6, Tiberius and another general, named Sentius Saturninus, led no fewer than twelve legions, drawn from bases in a number of provinces, against the Germanic tribal confederation led by Maroboduus. As the legions converged from Mainz on the middle Rhine and from several locations south of the Danube, moving toward Bohemia, the center of Maroboduus's domain, word reached Tiberius of a rapidly growing rebellion in Pannonia and Dalmatia that required immediate attention. Tribal leaders in Pannonia apparently saw their opportunity to strike against the Roman centers at a time when they were undermanned and when other bases would be unable to send reinforcements quickly, and they won many rapid minor victories. Tiberius and Sentius Saturninus quickly abandoned their marches against Maroboduus, and Tiberius moved his legions directly to Pannonia. These rebellious regions were only a short distance east of northern Italy, and Romans always dreaded the possibility of invasion from the north, having experienced such on a number of occasions since the early fourth century B.C. (see chapter 7).

Over the course of three bloody years, five Roman legions, some 25,000 men, battled the initially united forces of tribal groups in Pannonia and Dalmatia, in a region extending from the Danube and Drava Rivers to Macedonia. The military resources of Rome were stretched thin, with no extra troops available to move to the region and no possibility of raising new legions in Rome. Augustus tried, however, to organize units of non-legionary volunteers.

If Arminius, together with a unit of his tribesmen, did indeed serve with the Roman forces in the battles to put down this massive rebellion, the experience may have galvanized his determination to confront the Roman troops in his homeland. During his service in Pannonia, he would have noted two important things. First, Roman forces were overextended. Despite decades of successful conquests, the Roman military was now no longer able to expand its reach with ease. Second, native tribal leaders, observing Rome's military tactics and organizing large units of native warriors to confront them, could match the legions' prowess in battle. In fact, at one major battle at Sirmium, near modern Belgrade, in a landscape of marshes and narrow dry passages that seems eerily similar to the environment at Kalkriese, the native forces almost won a victory by launching a surprise attack while legionaries were preparing camp for the night. If Arminius was present in this battle, or if he heard about it soon afterward, it may have gotten him thinking. . . .

Youth and Early Service with Rome

Arminius was born sometime between 18 and 16 B.C. The year is uncertain, because it depends upon the interpretation of an unclear passage in Tacitus's writing about him. His father's name was Segimer, and the family was among the most distinguished in the Cherusci tribe of Germans. We know nothing about his mother. It is not clear whether the name Arminius was of Germanic or of Roman origin. The name certainly has nothing to do with the name Hermann, as he came to be called during the sixteenth century, perhaps first in Martin Luther's remarks about the early Germanic hero. Luther thought "Arminius" to be a Latin corruption of "Hermann," but modern linguists tell us that was wrong.

Arminius had a brother called Flavus, who figures in the historical account later, and an uncle named Inguiomerus. Arminius, like his brother Flavus, served in the Roman army, as we noted above. To supplement the fighting force of the legions, the Roman administration recruited soldiers from its provinces, and even from unconquered territories such as Germany, to serve in auxiliary units. Auxiliary units typically consisted of between five hundred and a thousand men, and during Augustus's reign they were usually commanded by their tribal leaders. In contrast to the typical legionary who was part of a heavy infantry unit, the auxiliaries were either light infantry or specialized troops, such as cavalry. In the case of auxiliaries recruited from the Roman provinces, such as Gaul or Raetia, the young men were drafted into the military and expected to serve twenty-five years. For auxiliaries hired from unconquered territories, over whom Rome had no direct control, the primary incentive would have been the good pay that Roman soldiers earned, but surely other personal incentives played a role as well, such as desire for adventure and to see the world. Arminius may have used his high social status among his people to organize a contingent of a few hundred men to join an auxiliary unit to serve with the Roman legions. He probably had a variety of motives for joining the Roman military. Besides earning a good salary from Rome, he would have gained considerable status, at least among those of his own people who supported alliance with Rome or who understood the advantages of creating the appearance of such alliance, through the special role he played in the imperial framework. And even from the start of his military service, he may have had his grand plan in mind.

During his years of service with the Roman military, he learned Latin, and in recognition of his contribution to the Roman cause, he was awarded Roman citizenship, a prize regularly bestowed upon leaders of indigenous units who provided exceptional service to Rome. Furthermore, he was granted status as an equestrian, or knight, a high rank in Roman society. He probably owed this honor both to his status within his tribal group and to his successful leadership in affiliation with the Roman army. Arminius's participation in Roman military campaigns as an auxiliary commander was to play a critical role in his ability to surprise and outwit Roman troops, when he switched his allegiance.

Around the year A.D. 7, Arminius probably left the scene of his service in Pannonia and returned to his homeland. His brother Flavus remained with the Roman military. Sometime in the following few years, probably after the battle in A.D. 9, Arminius eloped with the daughter of a rival member of the Cherusci elite named Segestes, a woman whose name was Thusnelda, who had been betrothed to another man. In A.D. 15, she was captured by Roman forces; shortly thereafter, she bore a son, named Thumelicus. Ironically, he was raised in Roman Italy, in the town of Ravenna.

Rebel and Unifier

At this time, the Germanic peoples east of the Rhine were organized into groups that we call tribes. The names of many of the tribes were recorded by Julius Caesar, Strabo, and other ancient writers. They include the Bructeri, the Chatti, the Sugambri, the Tencteri, the Usipetes, and the Cherusci, the tribe to which Arminius belonged. Tribes varied a great deal in size and in power. No overarching political organization unified all of the Germanic tribes of the region. The Cherusci were known as one of the largest and most powerful of the tribes.

Every tribe was made up of many villages and farms, and each had a similar leadership structure, consisting of a council of adult men who met regularly to make decisions for the tribe. In times of conflict, the tribal council designated a war leader, a man who had distinguished himself in battle and who showed leadership qualities. This man wielded considerable political power in wartime. Tribal borders were not as formally defined as a modern state's or nation's boundaries, and people could shift their allegiances from one tribe to another.

As a member of the most illustrious family in the Cherusci tribe, Arminius, though still a young man of about twenty-five on his return home to Germany from Pannonia, was better situated than most to lead his people. His military experience serving with the Roman army, and the special status granted him by the Roman authorities, gave him heightened prestige and authority. When he returned home, Roman activity was intensifying in his native land, around the headwaters of the Weser River between the Rhine and the Elbe. Varus had been appointed governor of the region, and he was setting about establishing the administrative framework of a territory conquered by Rome and being integrated into the Empire.

We do not know how long Arminius planned the attack on

the Roman forces, or what was going through his mind as he conceived and developed the plan. Some members of his tribal group, notably Segestes, were firm allies of Rome and favored absorption into the Empire. Perhaps Segestes and others like him were motivated by the promised benefits of joining Rome—citizenship and often cash and material subsidies for the elites, a position of authority in the new administration of the territory, and the material accouterments that accompanied alliance with Rome. Or perhaps they simply felt that the Roman armies could not be stopped and that it was better to ally with Rome early than to have to fight the legions later.

His Plan, Strategy, and Tactics

Thanks to his experience with the Roman army in Pannonia, Arminius knew how to plan and execute the attack. Arminius recognized that the Germanic tribal warriors could not successfully challenge the Roman legions on an open field of battle. Instead, they had to rely on their special knowledge of the landscape and on their greater maneuverability to attack their foe in its weakest position. Similar tactics were used by the American colonists in the early days of the Revolutionary War and by indigenous peoples in modern wars in Vietnam and Afghanistan. Knowing how the Roman legions marched in formation as they traveled, Arminius planned the assault in an environment in which they would be at their most vulnerable and least able to organize a defense.

Besides being a consummate tactician, Arminius was a leader of great personal charisma and authority. Even with the best planning and tactics, he still required many thousands of native soldiers in order to confront the three legions and their accompanying auxiliaries. To rally this support, he had to command the respect and confidence of the surrounding peoples. If the venture failed, the locals could count on severe and merciless reprisals by the Roman army. As it was, Rome launched savage punitive campaigns in the year after its humiliating defeat.

Basics of Life in Germanic Europe: Settlement and Economy

Despite what Roman authors wrote about them, the peoples of central and northern continental Europe practiced a fully settled agricultural economy, as their ancestors had for over four thousand years before the time of Arminius. They lived in sturdy houses in small settlements situated on rivers or smaller streams to assure a constant supply of water. Typical is a settlement excavated at Meppen, on the Ems River, about forty miles northwest of the Kalkriese battle site. Each of three farm complexes enclosed by a fence was dominated by a large wooden building that included both dwelling and barn. Each building was about sixty feet long and twenty-two feet wide, oriented east–west with a row of four large posts along the midline to support the steeply pitched roof. Two doors at about the middle of each long wall were marked by double posts to support the frames. Near the center of the house part at the west end was a round clay hearth about three feet in diameter. At the east end of the building were stalls for livestock, mostly cattle, together with some sheep, goats, and pigs. Each house was probably occupied by a single family—parents and children, and sometimes aunts, uncles, and grandparents. The importance of the family as the basis of society is underscored by the organization of cemeteries into small units of burials, accommodating close relatives.

Around the house-barns were smaller structures where the farmers stored grain and tools. Numerous sherds of plain handmade pottery represent the pans, bowls, plates, and cups that people used to cook, serve, and eat food. Spindle whorls—

weights that maintained the momentum of rotating spindles—attest to textile manufacture at the settlement. About thirty people probably made up this small farming community at Meppen at any one time. There were thousands of such settlements in north-central Europe, and the economic and social links between them made possible the organization of the military force with which Arminius confronted the Roman legions.

The farming communities such as Meppen grew cereal crops as their staples, especially emmer wheat but also other wheat varieties, as well as barley, millet, rye, and oats. Farmers used plows pulled by oxen. Most of the plow was made of wood, but a few parts, such as the share that cut through the soil, were iron. The plows were simple ards—implements that cut a single furrow through the earth. Plows with moldboards that turned the soil as they plowed did not come into use until the early Middle Ages. Around settlements were the fields where farmers grew their crops. In many parts of northern Europe, the field boundaries identified and studied by archaeologists sometimes indicate elaborate patterns of tens of fields extending out from the edges of the settlements. Fields were rectangular in shape and bounded by stone or earth walls, probably with hedges growing on top of them to keep wild animals such as deer out of the fields and to keep the livestock in when they were grazing on the stubble. The creation of boundaries around the fields at this time indicates that farming communities were intensifying their use of farmland—probably practicing crop rotation and grazing their livestock on fallow fields to regenerate soil fertility. The agricultural economy was well developed, being based on a wide range of plants and animals.

The people cultivated beans, peas, and lentils in garden plots. They grew flax both for its oil and for making linen. They raised cattle for dairy products, meat, hides, and bone and to pull plows; sheep for wool and meat; goats for dairy products; and pigs for meat. Archaeologists recover remains of all of these plants and animals and thus are able to reconstruct the food-producing and -consuming practices of the communities. In most communities, some people hunted in the woods, some fished in rivers, and others collected berries, nuts, and wild fruits. Bones of deer, hare, and wild boar are found on most settlements, and seeds of blackberries and raspberries, shells of hazelnuts, and seeds of apples, pears, cherries, and plums are common. But as in more recent times, these wild foods were only supplementary, providing no more than 10 percent of the food that any community consumed over the course of a year.

People stored their grain in pits in the ground, both for consumption in the winter and early spring and to serve as seed for the next year's crop. Many such storage pits have been studied by archaeologists, and recent experiments have shown exactly how grain was preserved in order to prevent spoilage. Peas and lentils could be dried and stored in ceramic vessels until needed. Livestock were, of course, available throughout the winter, and they provided the important dairy products that were much consumed during winter and spring months. To keep the livestock healthy throughout the winter and early spring, farmers harvested hay and foliage for fodder.

Much of the grain that people grew they ate in the form of gruel or porridge, or baked into bread. Milk was abundant, because most farmers had several cows. Cheese and butter were products of milk that could be kept for long periods and provide a measure of insurance against times that the cows might give less milk.

Besides water and milk, people also had juice made from the fruits they gathered from trees, and they made cider and brewed beer. Greek and Roman writers mention beer brewed from barley among these peoples of northern Europe, and they compare it unfavorably with their own Mediterranean wine. Other alcoholic beverages may have been made as well, such as beer from wheat, mead from honey, and wines from collected berries and fruits. Often the finest, most highly decorated ceramic vessels recovered on a site are the size and shape of a mug, and they are likely to have been the vessels from which the inhabitants drank their beer—like personalized tankards of more recent times.

In addition to plows, other tools used in food production included axes for cutting down trees and building fences, shovels for digging, sickles for harvesting grain, and pruning knives for cutting foliage from trees to use as winter fodder for livestock. Most of the farmer's tools that were in use in colonial America had already been developed by the late Iron Age nearly two thousand years before.

Domestic crafts common to most households included pottery manufacture, woodworking, leatherworking, textile production (wool and linen), and bone and antler carving. Many communities produced their own iron tools from local bog ores. By the time the settlement of Meppen and others like it were inhabited around the time of Christ, iron metallurgy had been practiced in the region for about seven centuries, and many blacksmiths were highly knowledgeable in the techniques of producing sharp and durable steel blades for knives, sickles, scythes, axes, spears, and swords.

The people in these communities wore jewelry that they made of bronze—earrings, bracelets, necklaces, and pendants. That metal had to be brought in from other parts of Europe, because the ores of copper and tin, the constituents of bronze, do not occur naturally in north-central Europe. Copper probably came from mines in the Alps, Carpathians, or Ore Mountains. The sources of tin are less certain, but prehistoric mines have been identified in parts of western and southern Europe. From the shores of the Baltic Sea, the communities imported amber, a fossilized tree resin that was believed to have magical properties and was a favorite material for beads and pendants. Other goods they imported, especially from regions to the south, included fine pottery, glass beads and bracelets, and silver and copper coins. For exchange, they produced surplus quantities of leather, furs from forest dwellers such as beavers and bears, dairy products, and perhaps preserved (salted or dried) meat.

Besides these long-distance contacts, the communities of late Iron Age Europe maintained close ties with their neighbors. In all societies, small communities such as those in the villages and farms of this region develop social rules governing the selection of marriage partners from outside, both to prevent inbreeding in a small population and to establish connections with other communities. We do not know the marriage rules that these villages followed, but methods now being developed for studying DNA from skeletal populations in prehistoric cemeteries may enable us to discern these rules in the future. Perhaps the young men in the villages of one valley sought their brides among the young women in a specific neighboring valley. In any case, it is clear that movement between communities was frequent.

The archaeological evidence of pottery, tools, and personal ornaments shows that goods circulated between villages, along with people. Though there were no paved roads and most people traveled on foot (horses were an expensive luxury for the wealthy, leaders of communities, and cavalry warriors), there was constant communication between villages. Probably members of families in neighboring villages visited regularly, just as we do today in our twenty-first century urban world. While we think nothing of driving fifty or a hundred miles on a highway to join family or friends for a weekend barbecue or dinner, the Iron Age villagers probably traveled no more than five miles, at the most, for their visits. Since in many areas villages were only half a mile or so apart, this was not a serious limitation on intervillage socializing.

Thus the peoples of north-central Europe, including those Arminius rallied in A.D. 9, lived in small communities, but they had well-developed agricultural and livestock-raising economies, they practiced a range of crafts that were important to their way of life, and they were closely integrated with one another, exchanging goods and sharing information. Even communities considerable distances apart were socially linked through marriage connections and other family ties, and perhaps several communities came together at certain times of year to celebrate seasonal rituals, such as those associated with planting in the spring and harvesting in the autumn. Although surely local dialects developed, probably the communities throughout a region could communicate with one another easily, as Danes, Norwegians, and Swedes can understand each other's languages today. These fundamental social networks provided the means for rapid dissemination of information that Arminius exploited in organizing the massive assault on the Roman armies.

Health and Life Span

The skeletal evidence from cemeteries suggests that people were generally healthy, but many suffered from problems that are no longer common in developed countries. Many people were plagued by parasites, some of which caused major infirmities, while others were hardly noticed. Dental problems, including cavities and tooth loss, were often severe. Crippling arthritis affected many older individuals. Except for treatments prepared from local plants, people had no access to medicines. Before the invention of modern antibiotics during the twentieth century, minor infections posed a genuine threat. Even a relatively small accidental cut from a knife or some other common tool could lead to death from tetanus, and farmers always ran the risk of puncture wounds from implements contaminated with bacteria that live in the soil. In combat, of course, most serious wounds led to death from one sort of infection or another.

Cancer is apparent on the bones in some burials, but cancer in soft tissues does not usually show up in the archaeological record.

As in most preindustrial societies, infants were at special risk

for infection, and probably some 50 percent died in the first year of life. Women giving birth were also at high risk. We find in many cemeteries that children and women in the childbearing years—groups most likely to die from infection—are frequently buried with charms, objects believed to provide magical protection.

Although mortality was high, many individuals survived to what we would consider a ripe old age. If a woman or a man lived to be thirty, she or he had a good chance of living to be sixty or seventy or even older. This point is important, because in nonliterate societies, the elders remember the community's traditions and histories and pass them on to succeeding generations.

Recent study of skeletons from cemeteries in northern Europe suggests that the average height for men in this period was around five feet eight inches, for women around five feet four inches.

Links between Villages

Communications between villages were important for many reasons. Young men and women sought their marriage partners in neighboring communities, and thus families living in different villages became linked. An especially skillful potter, blacksmith, or bronze caster in one village might attract customers from surrounding communities. When one community's crops failed, or a fire destroyed the grain stored for the winter, the intervillage connections could mean the difference between survival and starvation.

There were no paved roads in these regions, and all overland traffic moved on footpaths. (Paved roads north of the Alps—constructed with layers of sand and stone—were first introduced by the Romans in the lands that became their provinces.) Every village and farm was linked to all others by a network of paths,

beaten hard into the earth from the pressure of tens of thousands of human and animal feet, that had existed for hundreds or even thousands of years. The great majority of people walked, but wealthy individuals and merchants might ride horses. Merchants engaged in large-scale trade might even have a train of pack-horses, their packs loaded with cargoes of fine pottery, amber, bronze ornaments, fine textiles, and perhaps weapons.

But there are indications that communities could mobilize to join in the construction of wooden roads, or trackways, that opened routes across marshes. Many such trackways have been discovered and studied in boggy environments of north-central Europe, where the damp and acidic conditions favor the preservation of wood. Many were constructed as early as the seventh century B.C. These trackways represent the coordination of considerable labor effort, drawn from tens of farming communities, and indicate that a political structure existed that made possible the organization of such labor in the building of large-scale infrastructure that served the needs of numerous communities. One at Ockenhausen, near Leer, is eight-tenths of a mile long, consisting of about 13,000 wide oak planks that required the felling and shaping, by ax and adze, of some three thousand trees.

There were no major market towns in this region east of the middle and lower Rhine, though centers existed in areas to the south. Goods circulated between villages, carried by merchants, who might be full-time traders or farmers who became traveling merchants during the late fall and winter, when there was less work to do on the farm than at other times of the year.

Political Organization, Militarism, and Communication

Although settlements like Meppen were the most common in the lands east of the Rhine, there are many indications that changes were taking place, with the growth of larger communi-

ties and, especially, the mobilization of people from many communities to act in concert to meet specific challenges. For example, at Hodde, in Denmark, 180 miles north of Meppen, a much larger and more complex community had developed, with twenty-three houses together in an enclosed settlement, along with barns, storehouses, and ironworking facilities, with a population of perhaps 150 or 200 people (see illustration 18). One house is distinguished from the others by a more substantial structure, and the family that lived in it used finer pottery than the rest of the community. This change indicates that status differences were emerging and being expressed both through architecture and through household furnishings. Closer to Meppen, at Feddersen Wierde, just twenty-eight miles to the northeast, a new settlement was established late in the first century B.C. that grew rapidly in population and in productivity (see below).

Important evidence of mobilization specifically for military purposes comes from a bog at Hjortspring, on the island of Als off the southern coast of Jutland in Denmark. There a boat sixty-two feet long made of lime wood was found together with enough weapons to outfit an army of around eighty men. The weapons include swords, lances, javelins, shields, and chain mail—the earliest ever found in Europe. The character and numbers of the different kinds of weapons have been interpreted to indicate a highly organized fighting force, with commanders, heavily armed warriors, and more lightly equipped soldiers. This deposit of arms and armor, dating to about 350 B.C., shows that, already nearly four centuries before the time of Arminius, well-organized and fully outfitted military forces were organized to carry out targeted assaults. To produce a fighting force of eighty men, many communities must have contributed, and their coordination suggests the existence of political structures that encompassed many different settlements.

In the regions from which Arminius drew his troops, there is a clear indication in burial practice of the development of a new attitude toward military activity from around the middle of the first century B.C. on. Before that time, bodies were cremated and the burned bones and ashes either placed in a ceramic urn or simply set at the bottom of a small pit in the ground. Modest grave goods, such as a small ceramic vessel, an ornamental pin, a bracelet, or a pair of earrings, were often placed in the graves. Few graves contain much more material than others, suggesting that status and wealth differences were not strongly expressed in funerary ceremony.

Around the middle of the first century B.C., about the time of Julius Caesar's campaigns west of the Rhine in Gaul, a new practice of burying weapons in some men's graves spread in the regions east of the Rhine from which Arminius was to recruit his warriors two generations later. In many cases, a complete set of sword, lance, and shield was included, and more rarely chain mail and a helmet. A recent study of cemeteries in the lower Elbe region found that on the average around 10 percent of the graves in most cemeteries contained weapons. Of the weapon graves, about 30 percent contained the full set of sword, lance, and shield, while 70 percent contained only part of that set. Some of these weapon graves also contained bronze vessels—pails, jugs, or beakers—made in Roman Italy or in the Roman provinces of Gaul, and some included spurs, an indication that the persons rode horses.

The practice of placing weapons in burial sites does not necessarily reflect a period of increased violence, but it does indicate that weapons had become more important symbols of the identity of the individuals with whom they were buried. Funerary rituals are important in all societies, and in them communities express their deepest ideals and values. The inclusion of swords, lances, and shields in many men's graves after the middle of the first century B.C. reflects the enhanced symbolic meaning of weapons in the communities east of the Rhine.

The spurs in many of the same graves indicate something else of great significance. The Roman army hired auxiliary cavalry troops from among unconquered peoples. Already during his campaigns in Gaul between 58 and 51 B.C., Julius Caesar employed German cavalry in his battles against the Gallic tribes that resisted his armies. Since spurs first became common in men's graves that also contain weapons, and often Roman bronze vessels as well, it is most likely that these are signs of the buried men's service as cavalry troops in the Roman campaigns in Gaul. These spur graves thus highlight how entangled some individuals from east of the Rhine had become in Roman affairs in the decades before Arminius's great action.

An example is Grave 150 in a cemetery containing many hundreds of graves at Putensen, near Hamburg in northern Germany (see illustration 19). It dates to around the time of the Battle of the Teutoburg Forest. The cremated bone fragments in the bronze cauldron that served as an urn are the remains of a man about thirty years of age. In the grave were an iron two-edged sword, an iron scabbard, remains of a shield, and a lance head. Three pairs of spurs made of bronze and iron, and four bronze rein ends, link the buried individual to horseback riding. Unusual objects in the grave include a silver pin and six silver brooches. Two Roman bronze casseroles and parts of two local-style drinking horns were also present. The silver ornaments and four drinking vessels indicate the special status of this individual. Perhaps he was the leader of a band of warriors who served as auxiliary cavalry troops with Rome.

Two noteworthy points emerge from these weapon-bearing graves from the mid-first century B.C. on. One is that they suggest the development of a new attitude toward military activity among the late Iron Age peoples of north-central Europe at about the time that Caesar (who made two forays across the Rhine, in 55 and 53 B.C.) fought and conquered the tribes of Gaul. Military ideals and symbols grew in importance as the indigenous peoples felt ever more threatened by the advances of Rome. The other point is that the spurs in particular, but the Roman bronze vessels as well, suggest that some individuals in this region participated in the Roman military advances. Through such participation they became directly familiar with Roman fighting tactics, weaponry, and marching orders. In a very real sense, the Romans trained foreign soldiers who turned on them, using their personal familiarity with Roman military practices to their devastating advantage.

How Arminius Readied His Troops

Like Roman observers, many modern investigators have failed to recognize these profound cultural changes among the late Iron Age peoples east of the Rhine between the time of Caesar's campaigns during the 50s B.C. and the meeting of Arminius and Varus in A.D. 9. The archaeological evidence shows dramatic changes in community size, scale and content of interregional interaction, and military preparedness—what Nico Roymans has called a martial ideology. Weapons became an important component of male identity, indicating an increasing readiness to resort to militarism on a large scale. Men who had served with Roman forces in Gaul were identified by their spurs in the burial ceremonies. These burials are relatively common, suggesting that many Roman-trained troops returned to their homelands with an intimate knowledge of Roman fighting tactics and weaponry. The peoples throughout the extensive areas east of the Rhine were closely linked to one another through individuals who after death were marked in their burials by weapons, spurs, Roman bronze vessels, and personal accessories of silver and gold, as in Putensen Grave 150. The striking similarity of these burials—hundreds of which have been studied—in locations ranging from the east bank of the Rhine to Russia, from central Scandinavia to the Danube, indicates communication between these individuals, direct or indirect. Common goods and practices across wide distances show that significant information passed between individuals and peoples. Thus when Arminius and his co-conspirators planned their surprise assault on the Roman legions, they were able to spread the word quickly among hundreds of communities throughout north-central Europe and beyond.

In order to inflict a disastrous defeat upon the Roman legions, Arminius and his allies had to plan extensively well in advance of the event, and they had to draw upon men from a great many communities over a wide area of north-central Europe, because individual communities were very small. In Gaul, some of the larger fortified towns of the late Iron Age, the *oppida*, probably had populations of many thousands, and they were centers of often well-populated regions. When Julius Caesar's armies attacked those centers in the Gallic War of 58–51 B.C., the tribal capitals could readily muster tens of thousands of defenders. In north-central Europe, the situation was very different, because it lacked large population centers. But there were many communities scattered through the landscape. Fertile river valleys and the nearby terraces were often densely settled, while areas of poorer soils, boggy regions, and hilly lands were more sparsely populated.

Evidence from many parts of Europe suggests that there may have been a settlement about every half a mile, on the average. If we hypothesize, for sake of discussion, that Arminius and his allies drew on the communities within a settled landscape measuring fifty by fifty miles (probably an underestimate), with its center at the battle site at Kalkriese, then there would have been 10,000 settlements from which to draw recruits for the attack. If Meppen was average in size, then each settlement might have been occupied by 30 people, about one-third of whom would have been adult men capable of bearing arms. That would mean 100,000 potential warriors for Arminius's cause. Some observers would argue that these numbers are too high. If we assume a much less densely occupied landscape of one settlement every mile (probably too low), and an average settlement community of 20, then, leaving other estimated figures the same, the potential warriors would number around 17,000. The point is that, even with small settlements spread out over considerable territory, there were certainly plenty of potential fighters in the communities that Arminius and his allies could draw on to execute their attack.

7

WARFARE IN EARLY ROMAN EUROPE: PRELUDE TO THE BATTLE

When Arminius's warriors poured out of the forest in their massive surprise attack on Varus's legions, the two armies applied their distinctive military approaches to the ensuing battle. The Roman legions that campaigned east of the Rhine between 12 B.C. and A.D. 9 were the product of centuries of development in organization, tactics, and weaponry. They were the most powerful military force in the world at the time, and the men who served in the legions were proud of the traditions they embodied.

Their Germanic adversaries had behind them just as long a tradition of military activity, but it was different. Because they had no writing, we lack the descriptions of changes in organization that we have for the Roman legions. But from the archaeological evidence, we can examine weapon technology and military activity going back millennia before the encounters with Rome.

The meeting of the two armies in the forest and marshland of northern Germany was not as unusual an incident as the Roman accounts might suggest. It was characteristic of the confrontations between Romans and native peoples, especially during the Roman campaigns between 12 B.C. and A.D. 16. In fact, the historian Cassius Dio reports that Drusus came very close to suffering a similar disaster in 11 B.C., and Germanicus had some close calls in A.D. 15 and 16 (see chapter 11). What made this battle unusual was its outcome—the annihilation of three legions and a devastating blow to Roman self-confidence and imperial ambition.

Roman Warfare

DEVELOPMENT OF THE ROMAN ARMY

In the early days of Mediterranean warfare, from the late Bronze Age, starting about 1300 B.C., down to the sixth century B.C., wars were small in scale. Military groups consisted of men who temporarily left their farms and villages to follow a local chief in a raiding expedition or to defend their territory from invasion. Organization depended upon social relationships between the men who served as soldiers and their chiefs, and rewards included personal honor and booty captured from defeated enemies. In the *Iliad* and the *Odyssey*, the Greek poet Homer describes this kind of warfare, although the Trojan War was an event on a much larger scale than most conflicts—and hence the subject of Homer's epic poem.

During the sixth century B.C., the hoplite form of warfare was introduced into Italy from Greece, where the style had recently developed. Hoplites were heavily armed troops, with helmets, body armor, shields, spears, and swords, and they fought in tightly packed units. Swords and spearheads were made mostly of iron by this time, but helmets, shields, and body armor were of the more malleable bronze. This new technology and organization of warfare accompanied the growth of towns and cities, and it represented a more centralized and powerful military force. Hoplites were part-time soldiers. Typically they were land-owning men who were responsible for purchasing their own equipment and for being ready when called to defend the interests of their homeland. During the fifth and fourth centuries B.C., warfare became increasingly important for Rome. When bands of marauding Gauls from beyond the Alps defeated a Roman army and sacked Rome in 387 B.C., Romans responded with determination to establish a larger military force to defend the city and its territory. This experience also created in the Roman mind a fear of northern barbarians that loomed large in Roman thinking and action over the next eight centuries.

In the fourth century B.C., Rome increased the size of its military, devised means to enable the army to remain in the field for longer periods, and created the first professional fighting force to begin to replace the part-time warriors. The legions of the late fourth century engaged in some larger-scale warfare aimed not just at defense or capturing booty but at territorial gain for the expanding state. The legion consisted of three main categories of troops—heavy infantry, light infantry, and cavalry. The cavalry had the highest status and comprised wealthy men able to afford the horse and required equipment. The heavy infantry consisted of citizens who could afford the armor of that category. The light infantry represented the less affluent citizenry. The total number of troops in a legion was between 4,500 and 6,000, the great majority infantry, with some 300 to 400 cavalry.

As Rome defeated its Mediterranean enemies, such as Hannibal and his Carthaginian army at the end of the third century B.C., and expanded its domain in Europe, Asia Minor, and North Africa during the second century B.C., ever larger numbers of soldiers were required to make longer commitments to serve in bases far from the capital. By the first century B.C., the great majority of legionaries were professional soldiers, drawn from less affluent groups, both in Rome and in the rest of Italy. For many, a military career was an attractive option, promising adequate food and shelter, a cash income, and a social and legal status better than they would have had otherwise. To enjoy those benefits, they had to subject themselves to the often brutal discipline of the army.

Participating in a mutiny or deserting one's unit was punishable by death, as was failure to follow orders, though, at least by the time of Augustus, extenuating circumstances often spared a man. Minor offenses frequently led to flogging. When an entire unit disgraced itself by cowardly or insubordinate behavior, the infamous punishment of decimation could be carried out. The soldiers in the unit had to draw lots, and soldiers in other units killed every tenth man in the guilty cohort, typically by stoning, clubbing, or beheading. Although this punishment was rarely applied during and after the time of Augustus, numerous instances are mentioned in the written sources, and soldiers knew that the threat was always present if their performance wavered. And of course, even if a soldier followed orders perfectly and distinguished himself in battle, he always ran the risk of being killed or seriously wounded in combat.

Augustus made important changes in the Roman army and presided over new conquests of territory in Europe, Asia, and North Africa. His decisions regarding the deployment of Rome's twenty-eight legions were critical for conquering new lands and maintaining peace in the provincial territories. He stationed the greatest number of legions on the Rhine and the Danube, because those frontiers were the most important to his overall plans for Rome. At different times, five or six were based on the Rhine and six or seven on the Danube. Five were in Spain, three or four in Macedonia. Three were in Egypt, three or four in Syria, and one in Africa.

Augustus established pay and pension standards and set the period of service for the different categories of troops. By the first decade A.D., the usual term of service for legionaries was twenty years in active duty, plus five in the reserves as a veteran. Soldiers with the naval forces served in active duty for twenty-six years. Augustus's attention to the well-being of the soldiers, both during their service and in their retirement, was important for a number of reasons. It meant that Augustus could build the

Roman military into a large permanent fighting force of some 300,000 men, about half of them legionaries and half auxiliaries. He could count on them to provide good service when he ordered legions into action in different parts of the imperial frontiers. Since the soldiers were aware that they owed their good fortune in the army—attractive pay, relatively comfortable living conditions, a secure retirement—in large measure to Augustus, the emperor could rely on the majority of the army to support him in the event of any serious uprising or revolution. For his policy of imperial expansion, the good organization and high morale of the army were critical.

Supplementing the legions were the auxiliary troops—noncitizens from the Roman provinces and from lands beyond the frontiers. Auxiliaries served as light infantry and as cavalry alongside the legions, but in smaller units, typically about five hundred or a thousand men in a unit. Their pay was slightly less than that of the legionaries. The great advantage for the Roman generals was not only the added numbers but also the special skills, such as horsemanship, archery, or use of the sling, that the auxiliaries often possessed to counter the enemies against whom Rome was fighting.

Most auxiliaries were probably recruited in one of two ways. In some cases, rulers of native peoples who inhabited lands along the frontiers of the Empire, known as client kings, were obliged through their treaties with Rome to supply a certain number of auxiliary soldiers to serve in the Roman army, usually in Roman territory near their homelands. In other instances, native kings and chiefs in the unconquered lands chose to serve the Roman cause, and brought with them their warrior bands, in order to advance their own personal and their tribes' causes. Service in the auxiliary units of the Roman army brought considerable wealth and status. In the lands east of the middle and lower Rhine, Rome first introduced a cash economy, and many people were eager to participate by earning the wages paid to auxiliary soldiers. The leaders of auxiliary units, and sometimes the soldiers as well, stood to gain Roman citizenship at the end of their term of service and, if they won success in battle, heightened status among their own people. For many, leaders and warrior followers alike, service in the auxiliary forces of the Roman army offered various attractions.

From 15 B.C. on, Augustus's principal concern in imperial policy was the two-part goal of securing the Rhine and Danube frontiers and expanding Roman territory, or at least the Roman peace, beyond those frontiers into Germany. Accordingly, he concentrated his legions along those frontiers. Beginning with Tiberius and Drusus's Alpine campaign of 15 B.C. and continuing with Drusus's and later Tiberius's incursions eastward across the Rhine, Augustus oversaw more than two decades of aggressive campaigns into the heart of Germany.

ON CAMPAIGN

When Rome attempted to conquer the peoples of a new territory north of the Mediterranean, the generals led their legions on campaigns preferentially during the summer months, when the weather was driest and movement therefore easiest. Campaigns were carefully organized, and they followed a standard framework.

When they left their permanent bases, such as Xanten and Haltern, the legions marching into unconquered territory had to carry with them everything they would need in the field. The campaigns east of the Rhine typically involved two or three legions at a time. Together with auxiliaries, the total number of men was between ten and twenty thousand in each campaign. Soldiers marched with their own weapons, tools such as pickaxes for building camps, and personal gear in their packs. The legion's food supply, tents, artillery, and other equipment were hauled in wagons drawn by mules.

The arrangement of the units on the march was critical. Ease of movement was important, but in enemy territory defense was paramount. Marching order varied according to the terrain as well as to the disposition of the peoples who lived in the region. We have only a few descriptions of the order in which the different troops marched and do not know exactly what formations were employed in different contexts. One typical arrangement in enemy territory was to place auxiliary troops and cavalry at the front and rear of the column, and the legions in the central part, protecting the baggage wagons. Depending upon the width of the road or track along which the troops marched, the column could extend for a couple of miles. Under ideal conditions, the troops might march eight abreast, but when the track was constricted, hemmed in by forest or bordered by marsh, the column had to be narrower and thus longer.

On campaign, a typical day might have been something like this. At around 5:00 A.M. (when it already gets light in Europe in the summer), horns woke the sleeping troops. After a quick breakfast of bread and water, the soldiers took down their tents and then loaded them and other equipment onto the wagons. When everything was ready, soldiers and mule drivers fell into formation and marched out of camp.

After a morning of marching, in which they might cover as much as fifteen miles under optimal conditions, the scouts looked for a new site on which to pitch camp early in the afternoon. With their pickaxes and shovels, the soldiers hastily dug a ditch to form a rectangular enclosure, piling the dirt around the inside perimeter of the enclosure to form a wall. An attacker would first have to descend into the ditch and then climb up the far side of the ditch and scale the wall in order to get into the fort. Soldiers usually constructed a palisade of pointed stakes on top of the wall to create an additional impediment to anyone attempting to enter. After an hour or two of building, the soldiers pitched their tents inside the enclosure, following a standard pattern for each unit, looked after the animals, and began preparing their evening meal. After supper, there was time for relaxation, playing games, gambling, and fixing equipment, before bed. Soldiers had to share guard duty throughout the night.

The main food of the soldiers on campaign was wheat, dispensed from the supplies carried on the wagons and ground to flour by each eight-man unit. They usually baked the flour into bread or made a porridge, to which they might add small amounts of salted meat and vegetables. Soldiers carried an emergency ration of a three-day supply of hardtack (hard, flat bread made of flour and water), cheese, and salted meat. They drank water, sometimes mixed with a little wine.

At the time of Augustus, legionary soldiers were not permitted to marry; officers, by contrast, were allowed not only to marry but also to house their families in their quarters on the military bases. As has always been the case around army bases, Roman soldiers fraternized with local women, and we know that they often began unofficial families that lived in communities close to the bases. When the army left the bases to go on campaign, some of the women and children accompanied them en route. We have very little textual information about this subject, since the women and children were not officially part of the army and were of no direct concern to the officers, as long as they did not distract the soldiers from their jobs.

BATTLE TACTICS AND STRATEGY

The Roman army had developed, like the armies of other states in the Mediterranean region during the final centuries B.C., as a heavily armed fighting force designed for action on the open field of combat. The different categories of troops had their specific roles to play in the complex battlefield strategy, and everything had to be arranged precisely before the engagement began. The thousands of infantry troops lined up before an assault, they prepared their weapons, and cavalry troops took up their positions. These arrangements of soldiers, equipment, and artillery pieces such as catapults took hours to get into place. After the general was sure that everything was ready, the assault began with an extended barrage of arrows and large projectiles launched from catapults. Only after the front line of the enemy had been seriously weakened and thrown into disorder by the long-distance projectile weapons did the legionary troops move forward into battle.

Hand-to-hand combat between thousands and even tens of thousands of troops is difficult for us to imagine, because we have never experienced or even seen such a thing, though films and television programs provide vivid images of heroes slashing and stabbing their way to victory. Every battle situation was unique, and generalizing about the character of battles in which the Roman legions were engaged is difficult. From available descriptions and archaeological finds, however, we can piece together a picture of what battles may have been like. The ongoing excavations at Kalkriese are likely to provide much new information about Roman battle tactics, but more about that later.

The Roman legions relied on intimidating their enemies, with artillery barrages and other means, before a battle even began. Roman army units were often larger than those of the enemies they encountered, they were heavily armed, and they were highly trained. They offered a frightening prospect to their opponents. The vision of thousands of Roman soldiers, moving steadily forward in tight formation, all outfitted with sturdy helmets, huge body-covering wooden shields with ominously projecting metal bosses that could be thrust into a man's chest, stopping to hurl their javelins, then rushing headlong forward to stab at their opponents's abdomens with their swords, must have terrified most enemy soldiers. It is likely that many opposing armies broke ranks and fled, if not at the sight of the advancing legions, then at the first volley of projectiles or at the charge of the heavily armed troops. The advancing legionaries threw their javelins at the front lines of enemy troops from a distance of twenty-five yards or so, in an effort to frighten the enemy into fleeing, or at least to cause further disruption in the ranks before the two lines met.

Surviving written accounts of battles suggest that most Roman commanders were not notable for clemency toward their enemies. By the time of the German campaigns, the Roman army had developed into a highly efficient machine for killing large numbers of enemy soldiers. The use of long-distance projectile weapons at the start of a battle meant that substantial numbers of enemy troops could be killed without much loss to the Roman force. During and after battle, the legions' opponents were shown little mercy. They were usually killed rather than captured. Women from enemy communities were typically sold into slavery, but not the men. Roman commanders did not hesitate to order the slaughter of unarmed people. Tacitus describes the indiscriminate killing of men, women, and children of the Marsi tribe in their settlements and the destruction of everything in their territory: "eager legions . . . for fifty miles around, wasted the country with sword and flame."

What would seem to us to be the Roman troops' extreme violence and cruelty toward their opponents reflects an attitude shared by many Romans and fostered by public events such as gladiatorial spectacles. The Roman writer Cicero, who says that he finds gladiatorial combat "cruel and brutal," suggests that the shows in the arenas served the purpose of inuring the Roman public to extreme violence and bloodshed, the better to support the legions' campaigns beyond the frontiers.

WEAPONRY

By the time the major Roman campaigns into Germany started, in 12 B.C., the legions' weaponry was highly standardized. We have good information about this subject, especially from representations of soldiers on gravestones and from archaeological finds at military bases, now richly supplemented by the discover-

ies at Kalkriese. Roman weapons belonged to three main categories: projectiles launched at the enemy from a distance,
stabbing and slashing weapons used in close combat, and defensive weapons intended to protect the user from the weapons of
enemy soldiers.

The most important projectile weapon of the legions was the
javelin, or *pilum*. It had a small four-sided point at the end of an
iron shaft that could exceed a yard in length. This shaft was set
into the end of a wooden spear that was also about a yard long.
The javelin was heavy and its momentum concentrated in a very
small point relative to its total weight. It easily penetrated shields
and armor, and when it stopped, the iron shaft bent from the
weight of the entire weapon, making it extremely difficult to
extract.

Many auxiliary troops used spears with leaf-shaped socketed
points. Bows and arrows were also auxiliary troops' weapons, and
arrowheads are common on Roman bases. Slingstones made of
lead, stone, or baked clay were other auxiliary weapons that are
well represented on bases, as at Haltern. A soldier skilled in the
use of the sling could hit a small target at two hundred yards
without difficulty, with a small, but very fast-moving and deadly,
weapon (see chapter 3).

Besides the projectiles that Roman soldiers launched directly
with their own muscle power, the army also used artillery (pow-
ered by torsion, not by gunpowder). Wooden catapults shot
iron-tipped bolts, and ballistas threw large stones, especially at the
walls of defending enemies' fortresses. But the Roman troops
were unable to make effective use of any artillery pieces at
Kalkriese. Even if they had had such weapons with them, in a
surprise attack in difficult terrain, there would have been no time
to set up, load, and fire such machinery. It is unlikely that Varus's
legions even hauled the heavier, more cumbersome kinds of
artillery on this summer campaign. The Germanic peoples
between the Rhine and the Elbe did not construct fortified set-

tlements against whose walls the stone-throwing ballistas would have been effective.

After the troops had launched the various missiles, they moved forward to engage the enemy in hand-to-hand combat. The most important weapon at this stage was the two-edged short sword known as the *gladius*, employed by legionaries as well as auxiliaries. Its blade was up to twenty-four inches in length, and it had a long and specially strengthened point. The grip was made of wood or bone, and the scabbard of thin wood covered with sheet bronze. Scabbards could be decorated, and they had rings for attaching them to a belt worn over the shoulder. Officers' scabbards often had ornamental parts made of silver instead of bronze or iron, and sometimes they were inlaid with cut stones. Short-bladed daggers were carried by legionaries and auxiliaries as well. Both the sword and the dagger, in their scabbards, were suspended from a leather belt decorated with bronze ornaments. Long swords, more than thirty inches in length, were used by cavalry troops, which also relied on large lances, with points over twelve inches long.

For protection from enemies' weapons, the Roman legionaries wore helmets and armor and carried shields. Helmets in this period were most often made of iron, though some were bronze. They consisted of the bowl that fit on the head and a neck guard that projected from the back. Cheek protectors, attached separately at the sides, were hinged so that they could move freely. A band of metal across the brow helped strengthen the helmet against downward slashing strokes from enemies' swords. Officers' helmets had crests that held colorful plumes of feathers or animal hair, and these were supported by forked holders that attached to the top of the helmet. The crests made the officers easily identifiable on the battlefield to the men under their command.

Over garments that could include, depending upon the location and the season of the year, a linen undergarment, a wool tunic, and a leather vest, the soldiers wore one of four types of armor. Chain mail took the form of a shirt. Fragments of mail and the fittings that fastened the shirt together are commonly found by archaeologists on military bases. Scale armor consisted of small sheets of iron attached to the vest. Segmented armor was made of slabs of sheet iron fastened to leather straps. Full metal cuirasses— so-called muscle armor, because the sheet metal took the form of the body musculature—were reserved for officers and were some- times decorated with elaborate figures and designs.

Legionaries carried heavy rectangular shields, curved in the shape of almost half a cylinder. The shields were made of layers of wood and covered with leather. Over the hand was a round iron boss that could be thrust at an opponent's face or chest. The large size of the shield offered considerable protection to the sol- dier, and the expansive front was often decorated with symbols of his unit. Around the rim of the shield was a narrow frame of iron or bronze to keep the wood from splitting. Officers' shields often had silver or gold trim.

Hand-to-hand combat was exhausting. The legionary's weapons, including what he threw and thrusted and what he wore for protection, weighed around seventy pounds. Effectively stabbing and slashing at enemy soldiers with a sword while simultaneously fending off blows with the shield could have lasted only fifteen or twenty minutes in active engagement before complete exhaustion set in. When we read about battles lasting for hours, we need to reckon with advances and with- drawals, and renewed advances, not with constant clashing. It is difficult to imagine what it was like to be in the thick of hand- to-hand combat, with fellow soldiers falling around you and your own end likely at any instant.

Along with his weapons, the soldier also depended upon other equipment on the march. On his feet, he wore thick leather san- dals strengthened on the bottom by about 120 large-headed iron nails (see illustration 20). Although today we think of sandals as lightweight, casual footwear, the Roman soldier's sandals were heavy, tough footgear, comfortable on long marches. Besides keeping the feet open to the air, they permitted the soldier to march through streams and shallow rivers, because, unlike boots that would fill with water, they dried quickly as the march continued. In addition, the soldier carried a pack that contained rations, a cooking pot, and personal items such as games and ornaments. The loaded pack weighed about forty pounds. Combined with the seventy pounds of weapons, the soldier's load was a heavy one. Although soldiers did not wear their packs when they moved into battle position, if they were ambushed on the march, they might have difficulty removing them to defend themselves.

Officers carried some of the same weapons as the legionary soldiers, but their helmets were more ornate and their swords and daggers often trimmed with silver and gold. They did not carry as many weapons as the soldiers, nor did they carry heavy packs of gear. They relied on the baggage wagons to transport much of their equipment.

Cavalry troops were outfitted differently from the legionary soldiers. Their weapons were spears and long swords, and their shields were lightweight and oval in shape. The horses were often decorated with bronze and silver ornaments attached to the harness, and these included luck-bringing charms and bells. The Roman army used horses for pulling supply wagons and as pack animals as well. Mules, oxen, and donkeys also pulled wagons when troops were on the move.

MORALE

The men who served in the Roman legions were trained for a career of fighting, and their occupational and cultural worlds differed greatly from most of ours. They were highly motivated to stand their ground in combat and to perform their assigned duties. The centurions were directly responsible for guiding the troops in battle, and they earned their positions of command through their own heroism and effectiveness in combat. The soldiers respected them and did not want to let them down. Neither did they want to let down their fellow soldiers. As in most armies, the legionaries shared a strong sense of belonging to a community of soldiers. It was better to die fighting for the unit than to be among a handful of survivors in a lost conflict.

In addition to these values, which helped keep the soldiers loyal and obedient, more direct sanctions could be brought to bear. In the Roman army of the second century B.C., according to the author Polybius, there existed the practice of beating to death soldiers who failed in their assigned tasks. The harshest collective punishment for a unit that disobeyed orders was decimation (see above).

Most important in guiding the combat behavior of the individual soldier and of the unit was the set of values—bravery and loyalty—inculcated into the legionaries during their training and service. Individual soldiers, and units within legions, were sometimes singled out for special honors for meritorious behavior and rewarded with crowns, medals, or cash bonuses. These values were represented materially by the standards that every legion carried.

In every legion, a member of the esteemed first cohort carried a pole that had at its top an eagle of gilded silver or of solid gold, symbolizing Rome. In its claws the eagle often gripped thunderbolts, and in most cases its wings were spread as if it were about to take flight. Another member carried a standard with the emblems of his particular legion, usually including an animal, such as a bull, ibex, lion, or ram, that identified it. The bases of the poles had pointed metal tips so that the poles could be stuck easily into the ground. Every military base had a sacred place—a shrine within the principal administration building—where the standards were kept. Over their uniforms, the standard-bearers wore animal skins, especially those of bears or lions, to distinguish them from the other troops. The legion's standards were treated as religious objects and even worshiped; they embodied the spirit of the legion. The loss of a legion's standards to an enemy, especially of the eagle standard, was a profound disgrace to the legion and to every man in it. Such a loss could be grounds for the dissolution of a legion.

THE ROMAN TRIUMPH

When the legions achieved decisive victories, the whole of Rome celebrated a triumph (see illustration 21). By the time of Augustus, this ceremony was a well-established tradition. Like most public celebrations of accomplishments, the triumph served both to glorify the achievements of the victorious general and his troops and to reassert ideals that Roman society held dear. The triumph took the form of a grand procession in which the victorious general rode through the streets of Rome in a chariot decorated with gold and pulled by four horses to the temple of Jupiter. He was accompanied by officials bestowing honors upon him, marching soldiers of the victorious legions—one of the few occasions when Roman soldiers were allowed in the city—wagons bearing captured booty, and prominent enemy captives, in some instances prepared for public execution as part of the ceremony. The triumph was a grand celebration of Rome's martial values and of its confidence in its superiority over all of the peoples it encountered.

The Native Peoples

THE ROMAN VIEW

The Roman writers were not as well informed as we are about the military technology and organization among the peoples of northern Europe beyond the lower Rhine River. They judged the native warriors in terms of Roman ideas about military organization and practice. This fundamental lack of understanding of their northern enemies was one of the factors that kept the Roman legions from ever being able to conquer them.

MILITARY TRADITION IN IRON AGE NORTHERN EUROPE

The archaeological evidence makes clear that the traditions of warfare in northern Europe differed from those of Rome. Roman military organization was the product of an urban, literate Mediterranean society. During the time of Augustus, when the city of Rome had a population of about a million people, communities in northern Europe were much smaller and had no system of writing. Not until the Roman legions threatened them did these peoples organize military units of a size commensurate with the Roman army's.

The evidence suggests that when Rome was developing a hoplite-style system of heavily armed infantry, during the sixth century B.C., there was no warfare of such magnitude in northern Europe. Not until the time of the Hjortspring deposit, around the middle of the fourth century B.C. (see chapter 6), do we have evidence of concerted group military action, and even then the number of combatants indicated by the weapons was not more than eighty. Organizing, outfitting, training, and transporting eighty armed troops for military engagements attests to a certain level of political organization, but on a scale much smaller than that of Roman Italy. At Hjortspring and other weapon deposits of the time, the weapons are mostly of iron, no longer bronze. But bone was still much used for spearheads. The weapon assemblages of this period indicate that the great majority of warriors carried only a lance, usually made of ash, and a shield. The iron lance heads were up to sixteen inches in length. The wooden shields ranged in shape from narrow oval to almost square. Chain mail is well represented, with about twenty suits in the Hjortspring deposit. Short, one-edged thrusting swords, present in much smaller numbers than lances, spears, and shields, were probably the distinctive weapon of leaders of the warrior bands.

By the time that the armies of Arminius and Varus clashed in A.D. 9, the blacksmiths of northern Europe had further refined their weapon technology. Many examples of weapons and of warriors' clothing are unusually well preserved in ritual deposits of northern Germany and Denmark from a couple of centuries after the time of the great battle (illustrations 22–26).

Just as warfare in the Roman tradition was closely linked to ritual, as is apparent in the behavior surrounding the legionary standards and the ceremony of the triumph, so too in Iron Age northern Europe there was a close connection between war and ceremony. Many Bronze Age finds of weapons are in deposits believed to have been offerings to gods. The Hjortspring site is one of a group of such weapon deposits from the pre-Roman Iron Age, and many more are known from the Roman period, including Nydam, Thorsberg, and Vimose. An important change in ritual practice in northern Europe signals a response to Roman encroachments.

CHANGES IN RESPONSE TO ROMAN ADVANCES

During the final century B.C., important changes took place in weaponry, fighting techniques, and burial practices among the peoples of northern Europe. Many weapons of this period were considerably larger than those of earlier times, and the quality of the ironworking tended to be higher. Swords and lance heads were more often decorated. Long two-edged swords, up to forty inches in length, were designed as slashing rather than as stabbing weapons, indicating a change in fighting technique, adapted to combat between larger units of fighters. Lance points varied in form and size, with some as long as twenty inches. Shield bosses were made of iron instead of wood, and many were shaped with a point that could be thrust at the enemy or used to parry oncoming swords and lances. One-edged slashing swords, barbed spearheads, battle-axes, and thin thrusting swords were all in use.

Spurs are frequently associated with weapons, indicating the development of a cavalry.

As we noted in chapter 6, at this time the placing of sets of weapons in men's graves became common practice. To some extent, we can attribute this new emphasis on martial activity and military symbolism to the service of many young men from regions east of the Rhine with Caesar's forces in Gaul. Presumably the majority returned home after their mercenary service was completed. In addition, however, the societies east of the Rhine were becoming increasingly militarized in response to the growing threat of Roman aggression, brought home to them by Caesar's forays across the Rhine in 55 and 53 B.C. Their responses are apparent in new technologies of weaponry, larger quantities of weapons manufactured, and the increasing role of military hardware in ritual. The ever larger proportion of graves that contain weapons suggests that more men were becoming involved in military preparation and, hence, that larger military units were being developed. Since some of the men had served with Caesar, they brought with them personal knowledge of Roman tactics and weaponry.

MILITARY ORGANIZATION

Most of the weapon graves of the late Iron Age contain one or two lances and a shield, but about 30 percent of them also have a sword. Those with a sword frequently include other special objects, such as spurs and Roman bronze vessels. Thus a status distinction is evident in the weapon burials, reflecting the command structure in the military units. If we hypothesize that the men buried with just a lance and a shield were infantry soldiers, those with swords may have been leaders of units, and those buried also with spurs, Roman bronze vessels, and sometimes gold and silver ornaments were the higher-level commanders of the military forces. As with any organization, as the size of the units increased, more levels of command were required.

Slightly later weapon deposits in northern Germany and Denmark provide another source of information about organization. During the Roman Iron Age, it was common practice for the victors in military confrontations to deposit the weapons of their defeated enemies in bodies of water, especially lakes, as offerings to deities who had aided them, as at the earlier site of Hjortspring. At Vaedebro, in eastern Jutland, around the time that Drusus and Tiberius were conducting their campaigns east of the Rhine, weapons were deposited together with skulls and other bones from more than twenty humans. Some of the skulls and other bones show wounds inflicted by weapons.

Around A.D. 200, thousands of weapons were dropped into a lake at Illerup, in central Jutland. In the parts of the deposit excavated so far, 749 lance points, 661 spearpoints, 225 swords, 430 shield bosses, axes, arrowheads, and harness equipment for ten horses have been recovered. Of the 430 shield bosses, 11 are made of materials other than iron; 5 are made of silver and 6 of either bronze or iron with gold sheet ornament on them. The precious-metal decoration on these 11 shields, together with fittings for a small number of horses, are clear signs of status distinction within the military units. If we use the number of shield bosses as a guide, 11 specially crafted objects out of 430 may represent commanders, who constituted about 2.5 percent of the fighting force.

Environment and Warfare

Roman weaponry was greatly influenced by the army's contacts with the Iron Age peoples of Europe, particularly those of the southern parts of temperate Europe whom the Romans knew as Gauls. The helmets that Roman soldiers wore were derived from helmets created earlier in temperate Europe. The form of the long swords that the Roman cavalry and many of the auxiliary troops used was based on the La Tène sword developed north of the Alps. At the same time, the peoples of northern Europe borrowed ideas from Roman weaponry for the creation of new forms of their own—for example, in swords. Much of this exchange resulted from the mercenary service of Europeans in the Roman army. By the time the Roman legions clashed with the native warriors east of the Rhine, much in the weapon technologies of the two sides was very similar.

But in the realm of tactics, Roman and native militaries remained fundamentally different. The Iron Age Europeans did not adopt the open-field tactic of combat upon which the Roman legions relied, nor did they make use of heavily armed troops comparable to the legionaries. Their practice of warfare was adapted to the environment of northern Europe, with its extensive forests, marshes, and bogs.

The texts make clear that Roman commanders found the Germans' tactics immensely frustrating. The accounts of Drusus's campaigns between 12 and 9 B.C. refer to tribal groups' leaving their territories at the approach of the legions, allowing Drusus to march through unopposed, but depriving him of possible victories (see below). Roman writers observe that barbarian warrior bands attack ferociously, but retreat quickly, often in apparent disorder. The Roman commentators attribute these behaviors to the natives' inherently inferior abilities and their lack of organization. But it is apparent that the Germanic warriors knew exactly what they were doing. Their strategy and tactics were precisely adapted to their environment and to their enemy. Although derided by the Romans as inferior fighters, they frustrated Rome's efforts to achieve decisive victories east of the Rhine.

Rome's Military Expansion

The mythological date of Rome's founding is 753 B.C., by the brothers Romulus and Remus, who as infants had been nursed by a wolf. Archaeological evidence traces Rome's origins back into the Bronze Age, well before 1000 B.C., when farming villages occupied the hills of the later city. During the seventh and sixth centuries B.C., the communities there interacted increasingly with other peoples in Italy, including Etruscans to the north and Greek colonies to the south. Rome became an urban center, with a population of perhaps about 25,000, and another 100,000 in the lands around the small city.

From the latter part of the fifth century B.C. on, Rome began its expansion, first to the south into Latium, then northward into southern Etruria (now Tuscany). During the third century B.C., Rome undertook conquests beyond Italy. In the First Punic War, Rome unexpectedly defeated Carthage and won Sicily, which became Rome's first province. Through other wars, Rome gained parts of Iberia, Illyria, Greece, Macedonia, Asia Minor, and North Africa. After the Second Punic War (218–201 B.C.), Carthage ceased to be a Mediterranean power, and Rome dominated the western Mediterranean region.

These advances were interrupted by setbacks. Two in particular were to play highly significant roles in how Romans thought about the peoples north of the Alps and how they pursued their military policies against them. According to tradition, early in the fourth century B.C. the city of Rome was sacked by invading Gauls, or Celts, from the north. The story is presented in greatest detail by Livy, who was writing late in the first century B.C. According to his telling of the event, the invaders came across the Alps, defeated Etruscan cities in the Po Plain, in the north of Italy, and marched south toward Rome.

> As they marched swiftly and noisily on, the terrified cities armed in haste, and the peasants fled; . . . they signified with loud cries . . . that Rome was their goal . . . the Gauls . . . their wild songs and discordant shouts filled all the air with a hideous noise.

They attacked the city, rampaged through the streets, and set fire to buildings. Romans who had sought refuge in the citadel above the city witnessed the destruction.

Wherever the shouting of the invaders, the lamentations of the women and children, the crackling of the flames, and the crash of falling buildings drew their attention, trembling at each sound, they turned their thoughts and their gaze that way, as though Fortune had placed them there to witness the pageant of their dying country.

Livy's account was based on oral tradition concerning events 350 years before his time, and he surely added colorful details to the basic story. In writing his history of Rome, Livy aimed to warn Romans to be alert and to guard against dangers that might threaten their city. His story about the Gallic invasion emphasizes that Rome is vulnerable to outside enemies and must always be vigilant. His work shows how Romans during Augustus's reign remembered such events from their past and used the memories to fashion their responses to circumstances of their own day.

A similar threat developed late in the second century B.C. Roman historians record migrations southward of north European peoples whom they called Cimbri and Teutones. According to the texts, in 113 B.C. these peoples confronted and soundly defeated a Roman army at a place called Noreia, somewhere in modern Austria or Slovenia. Over the next twelve years, these marauding groups migrated westward into Gaul, then south into the Roman province of Gallia Narbonensis, plundering the landscape and repeatedly defeating the Roman forces sent against them. Finally, at Aix-en-Provence, the Roman general Marius was able to contain them and in 101 B.C. to defeat them for good at Vercellae, a place in northern Italy that has not yet been identified in the modern landscape.

The essence of these two historical traditions is the same—

dangerous peoples live in the north of Europe, and they pose a threat to Rome that can burst forth at any time. This theme was important to the way Romans thought about the peoples of Europe beyond the Alps. Both Caesar between 58 and 51 B.C. and Velleius Paterculus in his remarks about the Teutoburg Forest battle in A.D. 9 compare their subjects with the danger posed by the Cimbri and Teutones.

Julius Caesar, the Gallic War, and Forays across the Rhine

In 58 B.C., Julius Caesar began an eight-year campaign of conquest in Gaul (see map 6). In his annual reports on the progress of the war, Caesar indicates that he intervened to aid tribes allied with Rome that requested help in repulsing incursions into their lands. But his quest for political supremacy in Rome played a key role in his decision to intervene. In his account, Caesar mentions the Cimbri and Teutones no fewer than five times, drawing explicit comparisons between that earlier threat to Rome and the disorder in Gaul that he set out to quell. It is not clear whether Caesar actually believed that peoples in Gaul were a threat to Roman Italy, or whether he was playing upon the long-standing Roman fears about invasions from the north in order to win support for his military adventures.

Caesar began his campaigns in Gaul with four legions totaling around twenty thousand men, together with auxiliary troops hired from allied peoples in Gaul and Spain and even German cavalry troops from across the Rhine. By 51 B.C., he commanded ten legions, plus auxiliaries. The conquest of Gaul did not entail massive attacks on huge tribal armies. With troops from allied Gallic peoples, Caesar led his army in attacking the tribal capitals one by one. His campaigns culminated in a battle against the unified remaining resistance under the command of the Gallic leader Vercingetorix at the fortified hilltop town of Alesia in 52

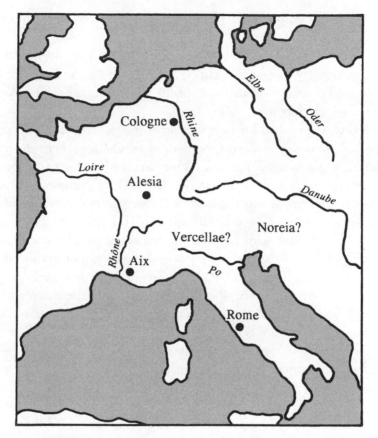

Map 6. Map showing places mentioned in chapter 7 associated with the migrations of the Cimbri and Teutones and with Caesar's conquest of Gaul.

B.C. After that hard-fought conflict, Caesar put down the last scattered remnants of resistance in 51, thereby adding this large and rich new territory to Rome's expanding domain (see illustration 27).

During the campaigns in Gaul, Caesar made forays across the Rhine, in the years 55 and 53. He wrote that German groups from east of the river had conducted raids into Gaul, and he wanted to destroy those groups, or at least discourage future incursions into Gaul.

His crossing of the Rhine into Germany had relatively little direct military or political effect, as far as we know. Caesar did not engage troops on that side of the Rhine in battle, let alone conquer any territory.

In 55, Caesar had his troops build a bridge across the Rhine, perhaps near the modern German city of Cologne, because, he wrote, it was beneath Roman dignity to cross the river in boats. The construction took his troops ten days to complete. After leading his army across the bridge, Caesar was met by representatives of several Germanic tribes who had come to establish peaceful relations with him. He treated other peoples less well. He led his forces into the territory of the Sugambri, who had abandoned their villages before his arrival and taken their possessions with them. The Romans burned the settlements they found and destroyed the crops (an action that would surely be remembered by the Sugambri and other groups), but did not encounter a local army. Caesar interpreted this fleeing before the advancing Roman legions as a sign of cowardice on the part of the German peoples, just as Drusus did later. This behavior on the part of the natives can alternatively be understood as a strategy to avoid direct confrontation with the heavily armed Roman legions on the open field of battle, trying instead to lure the Romans into situations in which the German warriors would have a tactical advantage. Caesar goes on to inform us that during his eighteen-day sojourn east of the Rhine in 55, warriors from different communities gathered to face the Roman legions in battle. But Caesar decided to retreat back across the Rhine instead of being drawn into a battle in the German forests, where his troops would have been at a severe disadvantage. His second expedition across the Rhine, in 53, appears to have had similar results. This time, he reports that although a force of Germanic warriors had gathered to confront the Roman legions, word of the strength of the Roman forces caused the native warriors to disband rather than engage the legions. Again, Caesar led his troops back across the Rhine to Gaul.

The aggressiveness and wanton destructiveness of the Roman army during Caesar's expeditions across the Rhine frightened and angered the indigenous peoples. Even before Caesar's first crossing, in 55 B.C., the groups east of the Rhine were well informed about the progress of Rome's conquest of Gaul. Throughout the Iron Age, peoples inhabiting the lands west and east of the Rhine interacted regularly. The river was not a dividing boundary, but a route of transport and communication. Boats had long been in use in Europe by the Iron Age, and it was easy for experienced boaters to cross the river. The incursions across the river that prompted Caesar's bridging and crossing of the Rhine indicate that those contacts were maintained, even with the Roman army in Gaul.

Caesar's description of the peoples whom he calls Germans is the earliest account of those groups that survives. He writes that the Germans do not have towns like the Gauls, or even settled agricultural villages, and that they do not practice any elaborate rituals. They are simpler and wilder than the peoples of Gaul with whom Caesar was becoming acquainted. He writes, "Their whole life is composed of hunting expeditions and military pursuits; from early boyhood they are zealous for toil and hardship. . . . For agriculture they have no zeal, and the greater part of their food consists of milk, cheese, and flesh." Caesar's statements of the 50s B.C. formed the basis for the subsequent Roman view of the peoples east of the Rhine. Later writers, including Strabo, Tacitus, and Cassius Dio, derived their ideas about those peoples from Caesar's, as did political and military leaders such as Augustus, Drusus, Tiberius, and Varus. Caesar's representation of the Germans had a very long life in the Roman imagination, and it still influences many modern historians.

Yet the Roman attitude toward these peoples was complex and varied. Despite his uncomplimentary characterizations,

Caesar hired German cavalry troops and light infantry to serve with his legions in Gaul. He considered Germans expert horsemen, known for their loyalty and trustworthiness as well as for their equestrian skills. Roman armies continued to employ German cavalry auxiliaries in different parts of the Empire long after the time of Caesar.

The Contested Rhine Frontier

Between the final phases of Caesar's conquest of Gaul, in 51 B.C., and the beginning of Rome's major offensives against the Germans east of the Rhine, in 12 B.C., the written sources about the Rhine frontier in Gaul are relatively sparse. Roman observers were largely preoccupied with other concerns, particularly the political struggles that followed Caesar's success in Gaul and the civil war that erupted after his assassination, in 44 B.C. But some important events were recorded. In 39 B.C. Marcus Vipsanius Agrippa was appointed governor of Gaul, and in 38 he successfully put down a rebellion in the southwestern part of the region. At the end of 38 or early in 37, he had to confront uprisings along the Rhine. In this connection, he crossed the Rhine into German territory, but we do not know either the reason or the immediate effects. In 29, the Treveri in the western Rhineland staged an uprising and called in Germans from across the Rhine for help, but Nonius Gallus, who was probably a legate in Gaul at the time, quelled the rebellion. In 25, Marcus Vinicius crossed the Rhine from Gaul to punish Germans on the other side, allegedly for killing Roman merchants. Agrippa was again appointed governor in Gaul in 19 and again had to contend with local uprisings, some perhaps aided by Germans from the other side of the Rhine. The frequent mention in the written sources of uprisings suggests that there was considerable unrest in Gaul during these decades and that many groups were not submitting peacefully to Roman administration.

A new phase in these conflicts began in 16 B.C. when invaders from east of the Rhine killed some Romans who were in their lands (we do not know why), and then crossed the Rhine to plunder. They ambushed a Roman cavalry unit, confronted and defeated the Roman Fifth Legion under the command of Marcus Lollius, the legate of Gaul, and captured the legion's eagle (see chapter 4). This defeat of the Roman legate and his legion, following several decades of internal uprisings and incursions by groups from across the Rhine, led the emperor Augustus from Rome to reorganize the defenses on the frontier.

Roman writers disagree about the significance of Lollius's defeat in 16 B.C. Cassius Dio represents the battle with Lollius as a disaster for Roman interests in Gaul. Suetonius portrays the event as serious, but not as significant. Some modern researchers view it as the turning point in Augustus's policy in Europe, when a fundamentally defensive approach to protect Roman Italy became an imperialistic policy of expansive conquest. Others, persuaded that Augustus had already made up his mind about conquering more territory in Europe, view the Lollius defeat as one of many events that hastened the execution of that policy.

Rome's Campaigns East across the Rhine

Augustus spent the years 16–13 B.C. in the Rhineland, Gaul, and Spain, directing the construction of military bases on the west bank of the Rhine and preparing the troops for campaigns across the river into Germany (see chapter 4). In the summer of 15, Augustus's stepsons Tiberius and Drusus conducted a successful campaign that resulted in the conquest of peoples within and around the Alps. Whereas we know about developments in Gaul from Caesar's commentaries, we possess no detailed information about the Alpine campaigns. That these seem to have taken only a single season suggests that the Roman armies met little effective resistance. Tiberius led his army eastward from Gaul along the northern edge of the Alps, while Drusus marched his from northern Italy through the central Alpine passes into southern Bavaria. Archaeological evidence for this campaign includes a Roman military base at Dangstetten, on the upper Rhine on the German-Swiss border, excavated in the 1960s, and the recently investigated site at Döttenbichl, near Oberammergau in the Bavarian Alps. At Döttenbichl, archaeologists have found hundreds of Roman military remains, all dating to around 15 B.C. They include three daggers, twenty catapult bolt points, over 350 arrowheads, numerous boot nails, and eight coins. Of special interest are three catapult bolt points marked with the stamp LEG XIX (see chapter 5), indicating the presence of one of the three legions destroyed in the Battle of the Teutoburg Forest twenty-four years later and never reconstituted.

The success of the Alpine campaign of 15 B.C. was of great importance to Augustus for propaganda purposes. He had a coin series minted to publicize this achievement. It shows the two victorious generals, Tiberius and Drusus, handing laurel branches to the enthroned emperor. In the summary of his accomplishments, the *Res Gestae*, Augustus stated that he had conquered the Alps from the Adriatic to the Tyrrhenian Sea. On the main road between Italy and Spain, along the Mediterranean coast of southern France, the Senate sponsored construction of an enormous monument to the Roman victories over forty-five peoples of the Alpine regions. At the apex of the 150-foot-high stone structure was a bronze statue of Augustus, with two figures representing captives beneath his feet. The inscription—the largest known from the Roman world—read in part, "To the Commander and Emperor, son of the deified Caesar . . . the Senate and people of Rome dedicate this monument, because under his leadership and planning all Alpine peoples from the Tyrrhenian to the Adriatic were brought under Roman rule."

In 12 B.C., another uprising is reported in Gaul, this one in response to the Roman census and taxation policy. Under Augustus, Rome established the practice of conducting regular censuses in the conquered provinces and assessing taxes based on both number of people and holdings of land. The taxes went to the city of Rome and were used to support the military, among other purposes. Not surprisingly, some groups resisted the Roman imposition of taxes.

As one means toward quelling discontent in Gaul, Drusus hosted a gathering of Gallic leaders at the Roman center of Lyon (Lugdunum) in southern Gaul to dedicate the Altar of Augustus in that city. The event highlighted Lyon as the Roman capital of the province and was a political gesture to win the acquiescence of the Gallic leaders. Later that year, Drusus repulsed new incursions across the Rhine by Sugambri and Usipetes and then crossed the Rhine into their lands. This action by Drusus marked the beginning of Rome's twenty-eight years of campaigns across the lower Rhine.

In the spring of 11 B.C., Drusus campaigned again in Germany, first attacking and defeating the Usipetes, then marching eastward to the Weser River (see map 7). Drusus was the first Roman commander to lead troops that far east in northern Europe, and he won great personal glory for this feat. While the purpose of the march to the Weser may have been to display Roman power, the action had an important unintended effect: it galvanized the Germanic peoples into organizing defensive strategies to fend off the intruders. On the march back from the Weser to the Rhineland, Drusus's troops were frequently attacked. In one place, they were trapped in a valley by the enemy and almost destroyed. Cassius Dio writes, "The enemy harassed him everywhere by ambuscades, and once they shut him up in a narrow pass and all but destroyed his army. . . ." The Roman legions maneuvering in this unfamiliar north European landscape were no match for local warriors who knew the coun-

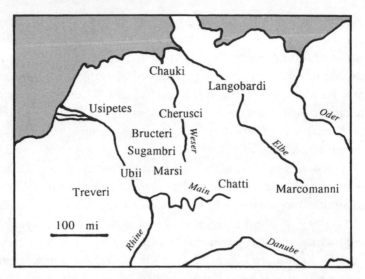

Map 7. Map showing locations of German tribal groups named by
Roman authors, according to modern interpretations of those writers'
geographical descriptions.

tryside. Yet, somehow, Drusus was able to escape narrowly with
the majority of his troops.

Drusus built two camps east of the Rhine, one at the confluence of the Lippe and a river that the Romans called the Elison,
the other near the Rhine. The first is believed to be the base discovered and excavated by archaeologists at Oberaden. Recent
study of the tree rings on wooden timbers that lined wells and
on oak posts in the outer wall indicates that the trees from which
those timbers were fashioned were cut down in the late summer
or fall of 11 B.C.—just when Drusus would have returned from
the Weser region and been preparing winter quarters for his
troops. Excavations at Oberaden revealed a large, multiroom
commander's headquarters building at the center of the base,
perhaps the residence designed for Drusus.

Again in 9 B.C., Drusus moved against peoples east of the lower
Rhine. Roman historians mention his attacks on the Chatti, the

Main Suebi, and the Cherusci. The Roman forces encountered tough resistance and lost many men. In following the retreating Cherusci across the Weser River, Drusus marched on eastward to the Elbe, "pillaging everything on his way," as Cassius Dio puts it. This demonstrated anew Rome's power and ability to move freely beyond the Rhine frontier. But the fact that Drusus led his entire army back westward rather than leaving a garrison at the Elbe indicates that Rome had not actually gained control of any territory through these campaigns. On the return march, Drusus fell from his horse and was severely injured, and he died of his wounds.

Augustus made great propaganda of Drusus's campaigns into Germany, including his crossing of the Weser and his marching to the Elbe. Official inscriptions implied that Germany had been conquered, and victory celebrations were held. Yet Drusus's actual accomplishments east of the Rhine were negligible. He seems to have regarded the Germans as no serious threat to the Roman legions (at least, such is the public record), and his lack of precautions got his troops into some dire predicaments. His long marches across Germany did little more than win glory for him and for the imperial household in Rome. The historical accounts imply that Roman losses were often high, though Roman authors did not write about them directly. The German groups through whose territories Drusus marched, whether they confronted the legions or avoided them, had opportunities to learn a great deal about Roman marching order and military preparedness.

After Drusus's death, his brother Tiberius took over command of the Rhine armies in 8 B.C. In that year and the next, he campaigned in Germany and apparently treated his enemies harshly. Our principal source of information about Tiberius's campaigns is Velleius Paterculus, who served as an officer in Germany and is considered by most modern scholars an uncritical admirer of Tiberius. In his account, Velleius portrays Germany as essentially conquered, and the later historian Cassiodorus, writing in the sixth century A.D., asserted that all Germans living between the Rhine and the Elbe had submitted to Roman power. But the reality of the situation in Germany was very different from what was suggested by all the imperial propaganda and the admirers of the imperial household.

Germany Pacified, Then New Unrest

In the year 3 B.C., the commander in Germany, Lucius Domitius Ahenobarbus (grandfather of the emperor Nero), whom Augustus had appointed three years before, reached and crossed the Elbe with his army. To mark this crossing of what had been a far barrier, he erected an altar to honor Augustus. Also under his command were constructed what are called *pontes longi*, probably causeways across bogs, somewhere in the region between the Ems and the Rhine. The very next year, conflicts between the Romans and the Cherusci flared up. The relationship between different factions among the Cherusci and Rome was complex and dynamic. While the elite members of one faction forged ties with Roman leaders, the Cherusci as a whole were to remain the most resistant of all the Germanic peoples in the region for the next twenty years. Although Ahenobarbus had accomplished the politically (but not militarily) important march to the Elbe and directed the creation of infrastructure in the region east of the Rhine, as a general he seemed no match for the Cherusci warrior bands. Augustus recalled Ahenobarbus to Rome in 2 B.C. and replaced him with a more seasoned military commander, Marcus Vinicius.

Six years later, in A.D. 4, Augustus sent Tiberius, who had directed a series of military victories for Rome, to the Rhine frontier as the commander in Germany again. Soon thereafter he sent positive reports back to Rome about his new military achievements.

Tiberius immediately undertook the conquest of a whole series of tribal groups, the Canninefati, the Attuarii, the Bructeri, and even the Cherusci, according to Velleius. In A.D. 5, he campaigned against the Chauci, then conducted a coordinated effort into the heart of Germany that involved both overland and riverine advances. The Roman fleet and the legionary troops met on the Elbe. Like Drusus fourteen years earlier, Tiberius departed from the Elbe to march back westward at the end of the summer without stationing occupying troops at this eastern position. All Tiberius accomplished was to demonstrate to his troops, to Rome, and to the German peoples that his army could move relatively freely through Germany without interference, but he did nothing to hold territory. Just as his brother had experienced, on the march westward toward the Rhine, the legions were attacked by German groups, but the Roman army seems to have defended itself successfully.

Part of the Roman strategy was to resettle troublesome tribal peoples, to move them to locations where Rome could keep better tabs on them and away from their regular allies. Tiberius resettled the Sugambri, who had caused particular problems for Drusus, in a new site west of the Rhine, where they could be watched more closely.

The Cherusci: A Special Relationship with Rome?

According to several Roman writers, the elite of the Cherusci tribe emerged as special friends of Rome after Tiberius's campaigns of A.D. 5. In the preceding years, a power struggle among different elite groups had resulted in the alliance of one party with Rome. The Cherusci were dominated by a ruling lineage that played a critical role in forging this friendship. The young Arminius, only about twenty-two at the time, belonged to this elite clan, and his membership in the group gave him a special position relative to Rome. Tiberius supported this ruling clan as a means of gaining control over this powerful tribe, and he granted the tribe a free status among the peoples of Germany. At the end of this campaign, Tiberius built a winter base on the Lippe River, probably to keep an eye on this important people. All of these special efforts suggest that the Cherusci played a major role in the disturbances that Tiberius had been sent to suppress.

Different Roman writers represent Tiberius's campaigns of A.D. 4 and 5 in different ways. Velleius, the officer with personal experience in Germany, emphasizes the battles in which Tiberius aimed to bring the Germans to heel. Cassius Dio, on the other hand, highlights instead Tiberius's and the German tribes' efforts at diplomacy to resolve their conflicts.

Germany Pacified Again?

Many of the Roman writers suggest that by A.D. 6 the German tribes had been conquered or otherwise pacified. Only the Marcomanni, under the leadership of Maroboduus, remained to be subdued. Rome planned the massive pincer attack mentioned above. But when word arrived of the rebellion in Pannonia and Dalmatia, the attack on the Marcomanni was called off, and Tiberius rushed with his legions southward to confront the rebels.

With Tiberius's departure from the German command, Augustus appointed Publius Quinctilius Varus to the position.

8

THE BATTLE

Creating the Killing Zone

In their experiences with the Roman legions, the Germans had learned a simple fact that indigenous peoples have known for thousands of years as they have faced better-equipped imperial armies. Small-scale societies cannot beat heavily armored forces on the open field of battle. But they can defeat them by attacking them in vulnerable situations, especially when they are on the move. Typically, lighter-armed native warriors, with superior knowledge of the landscape and greater maneuverability, can defeat heavily armed imperial armies in places where those armies are unable to take advantage of their technological superiority.

Arminius and his confederates selected a location in which they could ambush the Roman army at the end of its summer campaign season in northern Germany (see map 8). The place was the narrow track between the Kalkriese Hill and the Great Bog, a regular passageway that was easy enough for local travelers to negotiate, but presented complex impediments to a large marching army, especially after the plotters had made some alterations to the natural terrain. On the south side of the east–west route that led past Kalkriese was a row of low hills— the northern edge of the European central uplands. To the north was flat land—meadows, bogs, and ponds. A traveler walking or riding westward along the route around the Kalkriese Hill

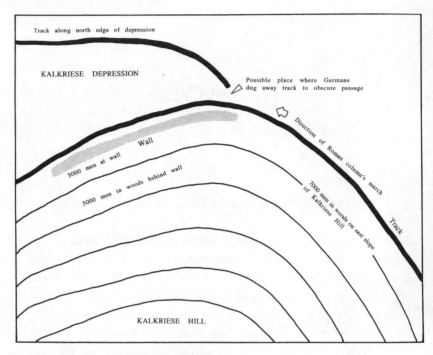

Track along north edge of depression

KALKRIESE DEPRESSION

Possible place where Germans
dug away track to obscure passage

Direction of Roman column's march

Wall

5000 men at wall

5000 men in woods behind wall

7000 men in woods on east slope
of Kalkriese Hill

Track

KALKRIESE HILL

Map 8. Map suggesting possible march route of Varus's legions and positions of German troops prepared for the attack.

would, at the northernmost point, either have to continue north
across the depression to the northern edge of the pass or bear
left toward the west, around the hill (see map 8). The Germans
may have created an obstacle to limit the Romans' choice, forc-
ing them onto the narrower passage. They may have dug away a
large portion of the track that led out across the depression,
exposing open water where land had been, and on the other
side of the water arranged brush and saplings to look like natural vegetation. The Roman marching column, coming around
the hill, would have seen open water there and no trace of a
track, then continued on the path leading around the base of the
hill toward the southwest.

To improve an already ideal ambush site, the Germans constructed a wall of sod that they dug from the edges of the track (see map 9). This project had two purposes. First, digging the sod enabled the Germans to narrow the track along which the troops would have to march, giving the soldiers less room to maneuver. The key to their plan was to confine the troops as tightly as possible, so that they could not use either the weapons or the battlefield tactics in which they had drilled. Second, the wall provided a protective barrier from behind which the ambushers could hurl their weapons in the first phase of the attack.

A team probably began by using wooden stakes to mark a fifteen-foot-wide and one-mile-long band along the southern edge of the track, following the contour at the base of the wooded slope. Then with long knives, swords, and iron-edged wooden spades, the workers cut sodden chunks of turf from along both edges of the track. They arranged the damp turves within the staked area to form the base of a fifteen-foot-wide wall. Once the base layer of turves was finished, they built another, slightly narrower layer on top of it, continuing upward until the wall was five feet high. Finally, they most likely cut leafy branches from trees in the woods to arrange on the front and top of the wall, so that the wall blended in with the hilly and forested slope behind it. Hundreds of people must have labored at this project from dawn till dusk for several weeks.

The Legions March into the Trap

The route that Varus's troops followed took them well north of the usual tracks along which the Roman armies marched during their summer campaigns, and hence into unfamiliar territory. For Varus, this was not an unwelcome diversion. He was confident that his predecessors had pacified this territory. He was glad to have a reason to march his troops through these more northerly

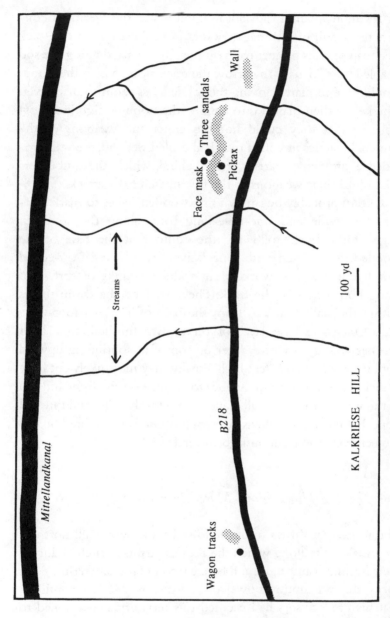

Map 9. Map showing locations of excavated wall segments (shading), some of the major finds, and wagon tracks.

lands, both to display Roman might to the peoples who lived there and to become familiar with another part of the region that was being transformed into a new province over which he would rule as governor.

When the army traveled outside of the Empire, marching order placed auxiliary units and cavalry at the front and rear of the column, and the legions, baggage, and commander with his retinue in the center. The width of the marching units of infantry troops varied from nine men abreast to four, depending on the terrain. If we pick a figure of six abreast for the arrangement during this march, take eighteen thousand as the number of Roman troops, and assume a yard between one man and the next behind him, then the infantry would have covered about three thousand yards, or a little under two miles. Allowing space for cavalry, baggage, and the commander and his retinue, and gaps between units, the total column length would have been around two and a quarter miles. If the march proceeded at the rate of three miles per hour (the mules pulling baggage wagons over the earth track were the slowest element), the entire column would have passed any given point within less than an hour.

As the soldiers marched along, they probably felt a variety of emotions. They were tired from the summer's camping near the upper Weser and eager to return to the relative comfort of their winter base at Xanten. Some felt excitement in anticipation of the welcome change in their daily routine that would begin in just four days, when they arrived at the Rhine. Many also felt varying degrees of fear as they trudged through the unfamiliar countryside. As they progressed, the landscape became increasingly wooded on their left, and on the right extensive dark and menacing marshes stretched as far as the eye could see. Many thought the dark forests and forbidding swamps were inhabited not only by potentially hostile natives but also by troublesome spirits. No Roman from Italy felt completely comfortable in the dark and wild landscapes of northern Europe, and memories of the close calls suffered by Drusus's legions still lingered among some of the troops. Frequently during their campaigns, soldiers swore oaths of devotion to the deities who protected them. Most wore amulets—bronze pins, pendants, and other decorations—on their uniforms to shield them from the malevolent local spirits. The presence of the governor Varus was important to the soldiers' morale. Knowing that the supreme Roman authority in this part of the Empire's frontier rode with them provided some sense of security.

As the head of the column rounded the base of Kalkriese Hill, the men at the front may have hesitated for a moment at what appeared to be a fork in the track. The beginning of a route northward along a low sand ridge seemed to lead across the watery depression. But it ended abruptly in a huge pool of black water, and on the far side was a thicket of underbrush. After the instant's hesitation, the lead troops bore left, staying on the narrowing sandy path that hugged the base of the hill. The edges of the track were cut away in many places, and soldiers on the two sides of the column were sometimes slipping into the muddy ground below the path. As they marched along, the men were forced to move closer together. In some places, only five could pass abreast, and those on the outside sometimes had to slosh through the swampy marsh at the edge. The scrambling of men to stay abreast and still keep their feet dry created confusion and irritation between soldiers jostling into one another. Some exchanged angry words, as one man's shoulder bumped another's chin, and the shaft of one legionary's javelin clanked against the helmet of another.

Meanwhile, the Germans waited nervously behind the sod wall. Some of the older men, who had fought against the Roman legions during the campaigns of Drusus, Ahenobarbus, and Tiberius, or who had lost kinsmen in battles with those armies, hated the Romans with passion and were eager to attack the troops and to kill as many as they could. But most were frightened, even terrified, at the prospect of confronting the dreaded legions in face-to-face combat. Like their Roman counterparts, the Germans had offered their devotions to the gods they worshiped, seeking protection in the battle to come. But those devotions failed to calm most of the men. They did not want to be there waiting for the Romans to arrive, and they did not want to kill anyone. But they had to join in this effort or risk endless ridicule, or worse. There was no choice but to make the best of the situation. If they won the battle, which their leaders assured them was a certainty, they would not only share in the glory but also win some of the booty stripped from the defeated Romans. For most, however, those prospects paled in comparison to their terror at the prospect of facing the imperial legions.

Arminius, with his experience in the Roman army and among fellow warriors at home, knew that most soldiers were concerned more with staying alive than with being heroes. He instructed his lieutenants to disperse the most experienced soldiers evenly along the wall, so that they might serve as examples to the hesitant and inexperienced.

Experience also told Arminius that his warriors would function better by using their projectile weapons from behind the wall against the mass of marching Romans than by engaging in hand-to-hand combat with those heavily armed troops. When they imagined facing the enemy, they could picture the six-foot-long javelins flying toward them, the deadly points piercing their chests, and they felt physically ill. The idea of rushing headlong into a line of Roman legionaries, set to draw their razor-sharp swords to slash a man's face off or slice open his chest, was terrifying. It was much easier to envision hurling spears from behind the relative safety of the wall at the forest's edge. If worst came to worst, there was always the possibility of fleeing back into the forest, however unlikely a successful retreat would be if the Romans were able to rally.

The Spear Attack

If we make educated guesses about the numbers of German warriors stationed at different places in and around the trap, we can
envision how the attack probably progressed. Working with our
provisional total of 18,000 men for the German side, let us place
5,000 along the wall, 5,000 back in the woods behind the wall
ready for the charge into the Roman ranks, 7,000 in the woods
on the east slope of the hill, and 1,000 stationed at various places
in the depression north of the track (see map 8). Along the mile
of the wall, one man may have been stationed every yard to
throw spears, and another two men behind him to hurl their
spears over his head, or to step forward into his place after he had
launched his. A man can throw a spear with accuracy every four
seconds. If, at the signal to launch the attack, every man began
hurling his spears, then within twenty seconds, as many as 25,000
spears could have been hurled at the Roman troops.

The Germans were well prepared with weapons for their
attack. Archaeological evidence shows that iron production was
widespread in the regions east of the Rhine by this time. Iron
ore, in the form of what is known as bog ore, was abundant in
most areas. Most villages that have been studied archaeologically
show evidence of iron production, and a few larger centers of
ironworking have been discovered. Most of the furnaces used for
smelting in this period consisted of holes in the ground, about
fifteen inches in diameter and twenty inches deep, with a circular ceramic chimney about a yard tall on top. At ground level, one
or more holes in this chimney admitted air, supplied either by
natural wind or by hand-driven bellows. Iron smelters loaded the
furnace with alternating layers of charcoal, usually made from
oak, and hematite or limonite ore, then set the charcoal on fire.
After anywhere from five to twenty hours, depending upon the
supply of oxygen, the quality of the charcoal, and the character

of the ore, the smelters removed the bloom—a lump of impure iron mixed with slag, about the size of a basketball—from the pit.

The next step was to reheat the bloom in another furnace to a red-hot temperature, then pound it with a hammer to drive out the impurities. The result was a chunk of wrought iron that could be hammered into weapons, tools, and ornaments. Well before this period, skilled smiths had already learned how to make steel. To create a steel blade on a sword or spearhead, the smith placed the weapon in a hot fire and surrounded it with charcoal. Carbon from the charcoal entered into the structure of the wrought iron to produce the alloy steel. Steel had the advantage over wrought iron that it was much harder and that it could be worked to a much sharper blade or point.

Archaeological evidence indicates that around the middle of the final century B.C.—at the time that Caesar was waging his war against the Gauls west of the Rhine—the manufacture of weapons among peoples east of the Rhine increased greatly. The change is apparent both in a rapid expansion in smelting and forging activity at many sites and in the new practice of placing weapons in the burials of many men. This increase in weapon production came in response to the growing threat of the Roman armies. In this elaborately prepared situation at Kalkriese, the Germanic warriors had a chance to put their expanded supply of weapons to good use.

When the Roman army marched through the countryside, scouts went ahead to make sure that the passage was safe. Why did scouts not discover this trap and warn the troops? The Roman army employed local auxiliaries as scouts, since they knew the land better than soldiers from Italy or Gaul. In this case, the scouts may well have been confederates of Arminius— part of the elaborate plan. They rode forward to Kalkriese, informed the men waiting there that the marching column was approaching, then rode back to tell the Roman troops that all was safe up ahead.

As the Roman soldiers sloshed along on the increasingly soggy sandbank at the base of the hill, the soldiers wondered whether the going could get any worse. Their earlier worries about malevolent spirits in the woods and swamps receded to the back of their minds, as they focused on staying on their feet and keeping more or less in line. Suddenly the men in the front third of the column heard piercing shouts from the wooded slope on their left, and seconds later a barrage of steel-pointed spears came raining down on them from out of the woods. The first shouts were echoed by tens of others from all along the trackway. These were the signals to the concealed warriors to launch their attack.

With no warning, hundreds of spears were falling from the air, or flying horizontally directly at them, and the tightly packed marching troops could do nothing to defend themselves. There was hardly room to raise their heavy shields, let alone throw their cumbersome javelins. Spears glanced off helmets and plate armor with sharp clanking noises, bruising the wearers and creating a terrifying sound, like huge hailstones pounding incessantly on a sheet metal roof. Some spears hit shields with a thud and a splintering crash, as they pierced the wood and often impaled their bearers. Even if the razor-sharp point missed the soldier, the shield became useless. It was extremely difficult to extract the spear in the midst of this assault, and the weight of the shaft made the shield impossible to maneuver.

Other spears found their marks directly. Some landed in soldiers' faces, some in their necks, others in their legs or arms. The armor of helmet and cuirass was designed to protect the legionary in infantry combat, not against intensive barrages of sharp projectiles traveling with deadly energy gained by falling from a high arc or being hurling powerfully at body level. The shrieks of agony as spearpoints penetrated flesh quickly drowned out the lesser sounds of spears hitting armor and shields. Wounded soldiers fell to the ground, many gushing blood and screaming or moaning in pain.

The cavalry horses were terrified at the sudden eruption of battle sounds—the clanking of metal points hitting armor and the screaming of men. When a spear landed in the flesh of a horse, the animal shrieked in pain and bolted, throwing its rider and charging off into the swamp, often trampling men in its path. Wounded mules tore off, jerking their wagons along, crashing into and bowling over soldiers, until the mules broke loose from their harnesses or collapsed in panicked exhaustion. Most wounded animals that dashed into the marsh became trapped in the deep mud and, weakened by loss of blood, soon drowned. Others charged in panic into the ranks of troops, trampling and wounding or killing many men. A few in their terror and disorientation bolted toward the woods, attempting to scale the brush-covered wall, often falling back into the ditch to die there of their wounds.

Within ten seconds of the start of the spear barrage, the marching units disintegrated into chaos. The attacked soldiers stopped walking, in order to try to defend themselves. Since they were marching in close formation and few could see much beyond the men immediately around them, those behind kept marching forward and crashed into their fellows. At first, soldiers farther back in the column were unaware of what was happening toward the front, and they kept pressing on. Like a chain-reaction highway crash, men piled into one another. Many lost their balance and fell forward. All the time, spears continued to fly into the ranks of the thousands of troops on the track in front of the sod wall.

When spears struck soldiers' arteries, blood gushed in little fountains, drenching both the wounded man and surrounding soldiers. Wounded, dying, and already dead men quickly covered the track, making movement increasingly difficult for the others. The scene was one of complete chaos—spears falling like hail, men collapsing and gasping, even those not yet wounded struggling to remain on their feet, and occasionally frenzied horses and mules crashing through the swarm of troops. Within minutes, thousands of Roman soldiers lay dead or dying, pierced by spears, while others struggled to stay on their feet and to raise their shields for shelter.

The Romans had no chance. In all of their training, they had been taught to fight well-planned, set battles on open fields. Once their order was broken, which happened in the first seconds of this attack, their command structure ceased to function and the units' maneuverability was destroyed. The seventy pounds of metal armor and weaponry, as well as the packs of personal gear, that burdened each man made movement to avoid the ongoing collisions between men and the continuing shower of spears very difficult. The heavy shield was almost impossible to raise effectively in the chaos. For most soldiers, there was no room to throw javelins. Only some soldiers on the south side of the column managed to hurl their javelins toward the attackers on the other side of the wall, but few hit the enemy.

Roman soldiers had been trained to remain with their unit, to fight for the common good, and never to flee. Flight and desertion were punishable by death. But in this fiasco panic set in. Despite their training, the troops were completely overwhelmed by the massive surprise attack in this terrifying environment. In their panic, hundreds fled. Most became mired in the bog, sinking up to their waists or necks in the slimy mud or, in some cases, over their heads, and drowned. Some thus trapped were quickly dispatched by lance- or sword-wielding Germans waiting for them on the edges of the swamp. Others were captured and taken prisoner, to be sacrificed in postbattle celebrations or kept as slaves. A few fleeing legionaries were temporarily luckier than others. They happened upon somewhat drier ground through the bog and, throwing aside their armor, weapons, and packs to reduce their burdens, ran as hard as they could away from the scene of the carnage. But Germans awaiting them on the bank at the north edge of the depression quickly killed or captured them.

Face-to-Face Combat

As the Roman soldiers tried to protect themselves from the shower of spears that seemed to come from all directions, struggling to maintain their footing as their fellows bumped and fell into them, amid the screaming, falling, and moaning, German warriors behind the wall felt a surge of wild courage and lust to kill. For the first time in their lives, they saw Roman legionaries—representatives of the imperial power that marched with impunity through their lands, bribing their chiefs and subverting their politics—powerless and helpless. Observing that the spears had done their work, throwing the infantry and cavalry into chaos and panic, the boldest of the Germans led their more hesitant comrades in rushing from behind the wall toward the nearest Romans, thrusting viciously with their lances. Most of the legionaries, bewildered, confused, terrified, and wounded, could offer almost no resistance. The German chargers, emboldened by seeing Roman troops at their mercy, lunged savagely with their lances, piercing abdomens and chests, and sending the front row of Romans staggering backward into the troops behind them.

Other Germans rushed in with their swords, hacking and slashing ferociously at the Roman soldiers. By this time, even the legionaries who had not yet been wounded by spears or lances were so exhausted that they could hardly manage to defend themselves from the sword assault. Germans slashed deep, mortal gashes into their enemies' bodies and thighs, hacked off Romans' hands and arms, and sometimes chopped off heads in their fury. Blood spurted everywhere, on Romans and Germans alike.

The narrow confines of the place played a critical role in the battle. Romans in marching formation had difficulty defending themselves against surprise attack in any circumstances. Here on the narrow track, bounded by the forest and wall on the south, and the marshy depression with open water and endless mud on the north, the soldiers were packed together even more tightly than usual. When they prepared for the type of battle for which they had been trained, Roman infantry soldiers had about five square yards of space in which to operate—to throw their javelins, slash with their swords, and maneuver their shields. On this track, under the spear barrage, they had very little space to maneuver anyway, and with the rest of the column still pushing forward behind them, that space continually lessened, and men knocked into one another and bowled over those trying to fight. The fallen, wounded and dying, presented disastrous impediments to those still standing, making their movement virtually impossible. In the chaos, they could not easily step over their fallen comrades, nor could they stand on soft, slippery bodies to fight.

Within five minutes, the entire passageway north and northeast of the Kalkriese Hill was full of dead and dying Romans. Yet there was no effective way that accurate information about this sudden catastrophe at the front of the column could be conveyed to the back. Communication between different parts of the column was severely hampered, because riders on horseback, who ordinarily could move quickly along the edge of a road to carry information, could not get through the densely packed troops on the narrow passage, nor could they ride easily through the deep, sticky mud at the edge.

After several minutes, word of the disaster made its way to the middle of the column, where Varus and his counselors rode. At first, Varus probably thought this was another irksome skirmish, perhaps part of the small uprising he was marching to put down—nothing more. In Syria, Varus had made his reputation by acting decisively when the situation required it, moving his legions into position to apply Roman power. Given what he had been told and had observed so far about the situation in Germany, he had no reason to think that similar decisive action would not win the day again. Varus ordered his legions to press forward all the more rapidly to aid their fellows at the front. He could not imagine the full extent of what was happening.

As the column advanced, crushing the troops under attack at the front, German warriors who had been waiting in the forest on the east side of the Kalkriese Hill swarmed down the wooded slope onto the rest of the column (see map 8). They ran fast, the front line hurling spears at the troops and rushing headlong with lances and swords into the stunned ranks of marching Romans. The entire column was now embroiled in battle.

The track, from the western end of the wall to the eastern edge of the Kalkriese Hill, had become a two-and-a-quarter-mile-long killing zone. The topography of the place did not allow the Roman troops to mass into deep formations, where their heavy armor and developed tactics could have been used to advantage. Everything about the situation was in the Germans' favor, and they killed savagely and thoroughly.

The German fighters had no such restrictions on their movements as the Romans did. They could range freely along the edges of the track, lunging, slashing, and stabbing at the hapless Roman troops. Heavy armor did little good when two Germans attacked one legionary, one from the front and one from behind, incapacitating him in seconds by stabbing their lances or swords into his unprotected neck, abdomen, or back.

At the sight of the thousands of warriors rushing down out of the woods, many more Roman soldiers in the middle and rear of the column broke ranks and fled, some to the north into the bog, others eastward, trying to go back the way they had come. Most were captured or killed. A few managed to escape and, by hiding in the daytime and moving cautiously at night, made their way, terrified, starving, and exhausted, back to the Rhine and the safety of the base at Xanten, where they told their story.

Varus realized quickly that all was lost for his army. Rather than face capture and certain torture and gruesome death at the hands of his enemies, he fell on his sword, a means of death that

Rome regarded as respectable—certainly more so than public execution after torture by the Germans. His generals and other officials did the same, in the knowledge that these northern barbarians delighted in tormenting captured Roman officers before dispatching them.

Once the soldiers learned that Varus and other officers had committed suicide, all remaining order disintegrated. Some legionaries fought like madmen, stabbing and slashing wildly at their enemies, but with little effective result. Others attempted to flee, now in all directions, since none seemed any more promising than any other. Still others simply gave up, allowing themselves to be hacked to pieces by their enemies, or taken prisoner for unknown futures—torture and execution, or slavery.

The battle, if we can call it that—"massacre" might be a more appropriate term—lasted about an hour. After that, all Roman resistance had collapsed. Many Roman soldiers were still alive but mortally wounded, and they lay, scattered and in heaps, on the track, along its edges, and floating in the marsh. Others had been captured and were being treated roughly by their captors. Some were still trying to escape through the marsh, but they were being rounded up by Germans on all sides, to be killed summarily or taken prisoner.

Some five thousand Romans had been killed in the hour during which the battle raged. Another ten thousand were mortally wounded and lay dying. A couple of thousand had been captured alive and awaited their fates.

Only a few hundred Germans were killed as the result of the feeble and uncoordinated resistance that the besieged Romans were able to offer.

9

THE HORROR:
DEATH ON THE BATTLEFIELD

To appreciate the meaning of the experience to the participants in the battle, we need to imagine what it was *like* to be there. We have no firsthand description of the battle, only the contradictory general accounts written later by historians in Rome (see chapter 3). For the thousands who died in the battle, the experience was the final one. But for the survivors—the vast majority of the German participants, the legionaries and auxiliaries who escaped, and the Roman soldiers who lived on as slaves in northern Europe—the experience of the battle had a vital and enduring impact. What they saw, heard, felt, and smelled during this brief, but intense, battle stayed with them for the rest of their lives. Their memories of the event, in all its horrors, affected their attitudes toward other people, toward warfare, and toward everyday life. Their memories of the battle came to play important roles in historical tradition, in legends, in myths, and in folklore. Battles are always powerful psychological and emotional experiences, as well as physical ones. Memories of the battle at Kalkriese survive in the historical tradition of Rome and perhaps in legends and myths from medieval times in northern Europe, such as the *Nibelungenlied*.

What Was It Like?

The battlefield was a scene of utter horror and human devastation that we can scarcely imagine. Razor-sharp spears careened off helmets and armor, or sliced into the soft flesh underneath the metal protectors. Men screamed, trying to wrench embedded spears from their bodies, at the same time that the surging mass of panicked soldiers crushed against them. Hundreds fell to the damp ground, pierced by spears or simply losing their footing in the chaos. Men shrieked in agony as the spearpoints penetrated their flesh, or moaned in pain as their lives ebbed away. Blood flowed everywhere, spurting from punctured arteries, and oozing from gaping wounds. Some spears tore open men's abdomens, and their intestines spilled out onto the blood-soaked track. The stench of blood quickly enveloped the entire landscape.

Once face-to-face combat ensued, attacking Germans thrust long lances into the chests, stomachs, and faces of disoriented and staggering Romans, and hacked madly with their swords at the outer line of legionaries. With freedom to move forward and back, and without the impediments of bodies covering the ground where they stood, the Germans had an easy time overpowering their adversaries. With their swords, they slashed at arms, necks, and legs, severing limbs and heads from torsos. The track became a mass of bloodied, mutilated bodies, many still alive but dying. Blood flowed in little rivulets across the track and down into the marsh, and all the ground was drenched in gore.

How Did the Soldiers Die?

THE WEAPONS

The Germans used mainly spears, lances, and swords to attack the Roman soldiers, and many carried light circular shields to ward off the legionaries' attempts at fighting back. But some wielded other kinds of weapons, different from those traditionally placed beside heroic warriors in their graves. These included prosaic implements, such as clubs, shovels, meat hooks, and billhooks— the kinds of everyday objects that peasants have always grabbed from their toolsheds when they rushed off from their farms to join in war. In the chaos of the close combat that followed the first minutes of the spear barrage, these everyday implements were highly effective in delivering punishing and often fatal blows to their adversaries. The Romans, who were restricted to a defensive role throughout the encounter, wore the protection of their helmets and body armor, and with their swords and daggers they attempted to ward off the blows of their attackers.

THE WOUNDS

In the battle at Kalkriese, the Romans and, to a much lesser extent, the Germans suffered three principal kinds of wounds. Spears caused mainly puncture wounds. The Germans' spears weighed an average of one and a half pounds. Thrown at a speed of fifty-five feet per second, they struck with seventy foot-pounds of energy. This energy was concentrated at a tiny point where the tip of the spear entered soft flesh, and the sharp edges of the spearpoint caused it to penetrate deeper into the body. Depending upon how hard it was thrown, the angle at which it struck, and the part of the body it entered, the spear could cause a shallow or a deep puncture wound. If it reached a vital organ such as the heart or lungs, the spear caused death quickly. If it lodged in the thigh or stomach, it caused a slower death through loss of blood.

Swords were used by the Germans at Kalkriese in a way that caused mainly gashes. Swords—short swords in particular—could also be used with a stabbing motion, in which case they could inflict deep and wide puncture wounds, but the evidence of the bones indicates that the Germans employed their swords mainly to slash and hack at their enemies. As with puncture wounds caused by spears, deep gashes into vital organs caused immediate death. More typical were slashes to the face, neck, arms, abdomen, and legs, that opened wide gashes, leading to rapid loss of blood. When a warrior chopped off a legionary's head, death was, of course, immediate. When he hacked off an arm or leg, the victim was immobilized, and rapid blood loss ensued, resulting in death in a matter of minutes.

The standard Roman sword—the *gladius*—weighed two or three pounds. Some of the German warriors had Roman swords; others wielded swords of various shapes and sizes that were current in northern Europe. Many of these were considerably larger than the Roman sword, weighing up to 4 pounds. The Roman *gladius* typically hit with an impact energy of about 100 foot-pounds, the larger German swords with two or three times that much. The razor-sharp blades of these weapons could create long and deep gashes in unarmored flesh. The large amount of energy that a heavy slashing sword delivered meant that it could also fracture bones.

Fractures were caused by severe blows rather than by cuts. Seventy foot-pounds of impact energy can break any bone except the skull. Even when the body is protected by armor, severe blows delivered by swords, clubs, or any other heavy implements can cause fractures. In the melee on the battlefield when the Germans attacked the Romans face-to-face, many of the legionary soldiers suffered broken arm bones, leaving them unable to offer resistance. Once a soldier suffered one or more broken bones, he was rendered helpless. On the trackway at Kalkriese, such victims became impediments in the path of their fellows trying to defend themselves, rather than making any kind of useful contribution to the Roman effort.

Deaths on the Battlefield

As happens in many battles, the losers and winners differed not only in the proportions of men killed and wounded but also in the types of wounds suffered and, especially, in the ways they died. In ancient battles for which detailed historical documentation is available, usually fewer than 5 percent of the soldiers on the victorious side were killed. Given the conditions at Kalkriese, the number of German soldiers killed may well have been even lower.

ROMAN DEATHS

The Roman soldiers probably died of three main, interrelated causes—destruction of vital organs, shock, and loss of blood. In the initial spear barrage, many spears penetrated legionaries' necks, throats, and chests, causing quick death by hitting the spinal cord, lungs, or heart. In the intensely savage lance and sword attack that followed, the ferocious thrusting of the sharply pointed lances and the slashing of swords easily destroyed the same vital organs and others, leading to rapid death. A lance thrust to the heart, or the powerful slash of a four-pound, razor-sharp sword that severed a legionary's neck, meant instant death on the battlefield.

Shock, or circulatory collapse, played a major role in the killing. Loss of blood is the primary cause of shock, but emotional stress also plays an important part. The horror of the initial attack, the panic set off among both men and animals, and the rapid wounding of so many troops created ideal conditions for battle shock. Many men lost consciousness and collapsed, some to bleed to death, others never to regain consciousness.

Loss of blood was the most common cause of death and was linked to the other two causes. The principal weapons of the Germans—spears, lances, and swords—all caused wounds that bled profusely. In the chaos of the battle, with the crowded and jostling conditions and the barrage of projectiles and subsequent swarming of stabbing and slashing attackers, there was no chance for a wounded soldier to bind a bleeding wound, much less receive medical attention from a fellow legionary.

Not all Roman soldiers within the killing zone died immediately. Many who were wounded collapsed to the ground, but remained alive for hours, if their wounds did not bleed copiously. Some who collapsed of shock regained consciousness. But once the fiercest fighting was over, the Germans probably walked along the edges of the track, looking for signs of life and killing any wounded Roman soldiers who they could see were still alive. Many of the wounded, partly covered by their fallen comrades, or lying in the middle of the track, lived into the night, to die of exposure. The next day, as they scoured the battlefield for booty, the victors killed any who remained alive.

GERMAN DEATHS

For the victorious Germans, the situation was different. Many fewer Germans were killed or wounded than Romans, because they had the upper hand from the start. Although occasionally a small group of Romans was able to rally briefly and beat back a pack of charging Germans, wounding and killing a few of these lightly armored warriors in the process, such incidents were limited and short-lived. Out of the 18,000 Germans who participated, perhaps 500 were killed by Romans fighting back and another 1,500 wounded.

Because of the different styles of combat of the two sides, the wounds the Germans suffered tended to be different from those of the Romans. The Roman legionaries sustained largely puncture wounds, caused by the spears in the initial barrage, by lances, and, to a lesser extent, by swords in the direct attack. Germans tended to suffer laceration-type wounds—cuts and slashes from the Romans they attacked, as these desperately tried to defend themselves with their short swords. Some suffered the same kinds of wounds that their Roman counterparts did—gashes and punctures inflicted by Roman swords. Much less common were fractures, because the Romans were so limited in their fighting space that they were unable to deliver the kinds of hard blows that caused such wounds.

Unlike the Romans wounded in the battle, almost all of

whom were subsequently killed by the Germans mopping up afterward, some of the German wounded had the chance to benefit from medical attention, depending upon the nature and severity of their wounds. With all of the interaction between German communities and the Roman world that is evident in trade goods, it is highly likely that some Germans learned Roman medical and surgical practices. Furthermore, when German tribal groups served as auxiliaries in the Roman army, some men probably received military medical training from the medical staffs of the Roman units with which they served.

The Roman military had a medical system that was extraordinary for the ancient world. It was based on the teachings of Greek medicine and emphasized both prevention—maintenance of conditions for good public health—and healing of battle-wounded soldiers. A nutritious diet, a carefully monitored water supply, and strict rules about sanitation helped keep the troops healthy. One result of this close attention to the soldiers' well-being was that Roman soldiers actually had average life spans longer than those of civilians, in spite of the dangers they faced in battle.

Gladiatorial combat in Rome surely helped inure Romans to the idea of battlefield injury and death. It also contributed to the development of highly skilled battlefield medicine. Doctors gained experience treating wounded gladiators and perhaps learned much about anatomy from dissecting those killed in the arena.

Medical professionals traveled with the legions and brought with them a variety of medical instruments, including probes, forceps, needles, and scalpels. Roman military doctors developed a special device that could remove arrows without tearing the tissue in which they were embedded. They created a surgical clamp that helped prevent gangrene. The most complex administration of medical treatment was carried out at elaborately provisioned hospitals at legionary bases, such as Xanten and

Haltern. Roman medical policy emphasized that in battle doctors had to get quickly to wounded soldiers in order to treat shock and halt bleeding, and this policy is credited with the relatively low death rate among Roman soldiers, at least in situations in which the Roman legions were victorious. At Kalkriese, of course, the situation was very different. The Roman army was not winning, and movement around the battlefield was virtually impossible. It is highly unlikely that medical personnel were able to aid wounded Roman soldiers in the battle.

For the Germans, the situation was different. Their wounded tended to suffer cut and slash wounds, often shallow in nature, rather than deep penetrations. Some German medical specialists had probably been trained to perform surgery and set broken bones, and they were likely proficient at staunching the flow of blood from wounds. Roman doctors carried out amputations when necessary and used drugs and herbs to help dull pain, and these skills may well have been transferred to their German counterparts. Thus many wounded Germans may have been saved by the attention of medical personnel who had been trained by Roman military doctors. But some kinds of wounds could not be treated by the available medical technology. If soldiers suffered deep penetration wounds, especially into the intestines or chest, infection, if not quick death, was probable. Severe fractures of the skull, especially if bone was knocked into the brain, could not be treated.

Many of the German wounded probably succumbed to the dreadful infections that accompanied many battle wounds in antiquity. Stab wounds from Roman swords would have been liable to become infected with tetanus, a bacterium common in soil abundant in the Kalkriese environment. Deep penetration wounds, and even deep gashes, if not properly cleaned, would very likely have led to tetanus infections and death. In several nineteenth-century battles, about 5 percent of the combatants contracted tetanus infections; of those, about 80 percent died. Approximately 5 percent of the wounded combatants in ancient wars contracted gangrene, another infection caused by bacteria in soil. Washing of the wound could reduce the incidence, and amputation might save an infected limb, but if the infection was not caught in time, death was almost certain. Blood poisoning was another danger, especially when a main blood vessel was hit and the spot became infected. This infection, known as septicemia, was less common than tetanus and gangrene, but almost always fatal.

Among the German victors, then, hundreds probably died of horrible infections in the wounds they received in the battle, days or weeks after the conflict. Others, with less serious wounds that did not become infected, recovered completely.

The End for the Combatants

The next morning, groups of Germans would have begun the final stage in completing the battle. By this time, animals had begun to devour the corpses that littered the track. Foxes from the woods tore at legionaries' flesh with their sharp teeth. Weasels and mice scurried among the bodies, licking at gaping wounds. Vultures and crows stood on the dead, tearing at their internal organs with their sharp beaks. Colonies of ants, beetles, flies, and other insects swarmed over the corpses.

Small parties of Germans walked along the edges of the killing zone, looking for any wounded Romans who had survived the chilly night. Almost all of the wounded had died of shock, blood loss, or exposure, but here and there the Germans saw slight movement or heard groans. When they did, they sought out the source of the life sign, and thrust a spear or sword through the man's chest, silencing him permanently. Within a couple of hours, all was still on the battlefield, except for gnawing sounds made by the larger animals and squabbling between vultures and crows.

Now the Germans were making their preparations for the victory celebrations.

10

THE VICTORS' CELEBRATIONS

The Battle Winds Down

The mile-long stretch of track in front of the sod wall was a mass of Roman bodies. Some were intact and some chopped apart, with limbs sliced off, and in a few cases gaping bloody holes where heads had been. Some bodies had been hacked open, and innards poured out onto the blood-soaked ground. About a quarter of the bodies showed signs of movement, as wounded legionaries tried to raise themselves or turn over. The rest were motionless. Thousands of soldiers had fallen here, and in places they lay two and three deep. Everything was covered with blood, streams of which ran northward down into the marsh toward the Great Bog. Severed limbs lay between and on top of bodies, and disembodied heads between corpses. Bent and bloody swords and spears were scattered between, on, and sticking into other corpses. Splintered shields littered the landscape. Legionaries' packs and the men's personal effects were strewn everywhere, and they too were covered with blood. Hacked and bleeding bodies of mules and horses formed gray and brown masses above the rest of the debris.

To the east, where the middle and rear portions of the column had been marching when the attack began, the corpses were more widely scattered. Since the attack there struck a few minutes later, and since they were not yet in the narrow passage bounded by the wall and the marsh, more Romans in those parts of the column had attempted to flee. Many hundreds of bodies were scattered to the north throughout the marsh, some floating in pools, others sprawled on grassy banks above the water. Germans concealed in the bushes by the edge of the swamp raced after them as they fled, hurling spears into them at short range or hacking them to pieces with their swords. Other corpses lay farther east, where men had tried to run away in the direction from which they had come on their march, only to encounter bands of Germans waiting by the edge of the woods east of the Kalkriese Hill.

Altogether some 17,000 bodies littered the track and the southern edges of the marsh, about 16,000 those of Roman legionaries and their auxiliaries. Their equipment was scattered about them—16,000 swords, daggers, helmets, and suits of armor, and nearly 25,000 javelins, most of which had not been thrown. Bronze pans, iron tools, bronze and silver coins, and personal items were strewn everywhere.

After the Battle

As the battle wound down, the victors began their postbattle mop-up operations. These included caring for their own wounded, removing their dead from the battlefield, and killing any Romans who still showed signs of life. Some German warriors who remained alive had suffered terrible gashes to the abdomen or legs that rendered them immobile, and they lay on the battlefield among the Roman dead. They called out for help when their fellows approached. Their comrades bandaged their wounds as well as they could and carried them to the edge of the woods for washing and medical care. A couple of hundred probably suffered these kinds of wounds. Some would recover, while others would die soon of loss of blood, or later of infection.

Like the Roman troops, the German fighters had among them men trained in military medical treatment. They combined traditional practices with techniques learned from Roman doctors during their service with the auxiliary forces in the Roman army. As the wounded Germans were carried off the battlefield, they were brought to a few central places behind the wall at the edge of the woods, where their medical specialists examined and aided them. They were practiced at washing gashes and stab wounds with clear, clean water and at setting broken limb bones. They knew how to make bandages of tree bark and leather and how to use herbs to ease pain and to restore the balance of humors—the bodily fluids upon which life and good health were believed to depend.

After removing their wounded from the battlefield, the Germans who were still able returned to retrieve their dead. They dragged some off the track by their arms, others they carried, placing the bodies next to the sod wall or by the edge of the track. They were always careful to collect the weapons next to their fallen comrades. The dead would receive funerary rituals deserved by heroes fighting for their own people; and it was important to include their weapons with them in the grave. Men from the different communities walked along the edge of the killing zone, identifying their own dead for transportation back home for funerary celebrations.

By this time—two hours after the start of the battle, an hour after its conclusion—of the sixteen thousand Romans lying on the site, perhaps a thousand were still alive, though too severely wounded to flee. Many were dying from loss of blood and shock. After they had removed their wounded to be cared for by those skilled in the healing arts, and their dead for funerary rituals, the still-strong Germans returned to the battlefield to finish off any Romans who were still alive and to begin the process of removing weapons and equipment from the enemy dead. Wounded Romans were dispatched with a spear thrust through the neck or heart, or simply left to die in the night from exposure.

The Funerary Rituals

The next day, men from the hundreds of communities that had joined in the battle began the treks back to their homes, carrying their dead on horses, carts, or hastily made litters. In the villages, the returnees were greeted by the women, children, and old men with joy and celebration, tinged with deep sorrow for those lost in the fight. All came to view the bodies of the fallen heroes. The next day, or a day or two later in the case of fighters who had traveled far to join the attack, in every village that suffered the loss of one or more men, funeral pyres were built of branches and logs. The rituals varied somewhat in different communities. In a typical ceremony, the body was placed on top of the pile of fuel, and the local elder or a person especially versed in ritual tradition spoke to the assembled community of the man's sacrifice for his people, as all attending bowed their heads in respect. Then the man's wife or eldest child touched a burning taper to the tinder at the base of the pyre, and the body was cremated in a solemn ceremony.

Treatment of the cremated remains varied. Although every community had rules and customs that were recognized by all, each family was permitted to practice variations on the standard procedures. In many cases, after several hours of burning and smoldering, the burned bones and ashes were gathered up and placed in a vessel, most often an urn of local pottery, but sometimes a bronze cauldron that had been acquired through trade from traveling merchants and treasured by the family.

The weapons of the fallen heroes were important elements in the funerary celebrations and in the creation of the grave. Sometimes the man's sword and a spear or two were arranged next to his corpse on the funeral pyre and thus damaged by the fire, but more often they were placed in the grave unburned. Typically, one of the participants in the funeral bent the sword, so that it could never again be used by anyone—in effect, killing it to go into eternity with its hero. With all members of the community in attendance, the urn containing the cremated remains was lowered into a hole in the ground, and the sword, spearhead, and sometimes parts of a shield were arranged around the urn. Then the soil was slowly pushed back into the hole, covering the urn and the weapons, as the mourners wept.

Sacrificing Prisoners

In the later stages of the battle, when it was clear that the Romans were defeated, the Germans took about fifteen hundred prisoners. It was the custom among the Germanic peoples to sacrifice some of the captured members of the enemy army as offerings to their gods, and with the defeat of the feared Roman legions, this practice took on an especially powerful meaning. But the need to perform this ritual had to be balanced with the practical desire to keep some prisoners as slaves, for retention by warriors who had distinguished themselves in combat. Let us suppose that Arminius and the other leaders agreed to select five hundred men for sacrifice and keep the remaining thousand as slaves. This would have been a high number for sacrifice, but the Roman army was much hated for all of its marching through their lands and for the Romans' presumption that the Germans were easy prey for conquest. Watching and participating in the sacrifice of Roman soldiers—especially centurions—would delight the victorious fighters, and the gods would be greatly pleased with the sacrifices, particularly those of officers.

For the night after the battle, the five hundred Romans to be sacrificed may have been herded into parts of the ditch in front of the sod wall and bound with cords. Guards were posted to be sure none loosened their bonds and escaped. At first light, preparations were made for the celebratory ceremonies of offering.

The Germans believed that their gods liked to see their victims die in different ways, particularly ways that were not quick and merciful. For the varied rituals, some were led into the forest, others down to the marsh.

In the forest, groups of Germans had prepared sacrificial altars—rectangular enclosures about five square yards in area marked out by stones. Some of the Roman officers were dragged, one at a time, into these spaces. In front of a crowd of enthusiastic warriors, a German leader recited an incantation to a particular deity, joined in parts by those surrounding the altar, then slashed the victim's throat with a sharp knife. The victim collapsed, his throat gushing blood. The body was dragged aside, and the next victim was hauled into the enclosure.

Others were hanged from trees, especially oaks. The Germans threw a rope over the lowest branch of a large oak tree, and tied a noose in one end. A Roman soldier was dragged to the base of the tree, and the noose was looped over his head and tightened. Five Germans held on to the other end. After one man said a few sentences of offering to a deity, the five pulled on the rope as they walked away from the tree, lifting the doomed Roman soldier off the ground. The victim writhed wildly and made ghastly gasping and choking noises, to the amusement of the crowd of taunting Germans witnessing the spectacle. After a couple of minutes, the body hung limp. The men on the other end of the rope let the body down. The noose was loosened and lifted over the dead man's head. The body was hauled aside to be left in the woods, and the next victim was dragged forward.

With their long swords, Germans chopped the heads off some of the sacrificed legionaries and fastened them to trees. One held the head against the trunk while another used a wooden mallet to pound a foot-long spike through one eye and the brain and out the back of the skull. These bloody heads nailed to trees created a ghastly and terrifying atmosphere for the Romans who were being dragged to their doom, but for the Germans they decorated a sacred temple of victory in their beloved dark, quiet woods.

Other Roman soldiers were sacrificed in the marshes, in honor of gods who dwelt in the murky waters. Groups of Germans assembled at the edges of dark pools of open water. They hauled bound Roman captives forward, one at a time. One of the Germans might slash the victim's throat, and others held the victim over the edge of the pool, his blood spouting from his neck into the dark water. When the flow of blood slowed, they hurled the motionless corpse into the pool. The Germans stabbed others in the heart, allowing the gushing blood to pour into the pool, then dumped the lifeless body into the water.

The sacrificing of the five hundred Roman officers and legionaries took most of the morning.

Plunder and Offering

As they finished carrying out the other tasks after the end of the battle, the victors began walking across the battlefield and collecting the weapons, armor, bronze vessels, coins, personal ornaments, and anything else they could see and easily retrieve. They felt elated as they twisted swords from dead legionaries' hands, yanked daggers from their scabbards, and wrenched helmets from their heads. These objects were treasured and indeed sacred symbols—prizes that stood as emblems of the martial success of these tribal warriors over the hated Roman legions.

In gratitude to the gods of war from whom they had sought supplication before the battle, and who had abundantly favored them in the action (and also to increase the likelihood that they would favor them again next time), the victors sacrificed most of the booty as their sacred offerings. There was excitement and satisfaction as they gathered their treasures and carried them to great heaps along the edges of the killing zone. As the mounds of

Roman weapons and ornaments grew higher, the German warriors became increasingly excited and jubilant.

The rules of German warfare stipulated that military victories be celebrated by the common sacrifice of some of the weapons of the defeated army—and of surviving members of that army—to the martial gods. But custom permitted the retaining of other captured weapons, to be distributed to the warriors who had contributed to the victory. The fine Roman legionary swords and the ornate officers' daggers were particularly valued. Those honored with these prizes kept them as personal trophies, or used them as high-status items to exchange with trade partners in other communities. During the collecting of weapons and other Roman goods, some men ripped pieces of sheet gold and silver off iron weapons, concealing the precious metal on their persons and depositing the base metal onto the growing piles.

For the Germans of northern Europe, forests and bodies of water had always been especially sacred. These were places where they carried out rituals, and both were inhabited by nature spirits. In forests, groves of trees that were set apart from others were highly attractive for ritual, particularly groves of oaks. Even though all water was sacred, still black pools were deemed most potent, such as those common in great marshes and the isolated ponds in forests. Archaeological evidence shows that these ritual practices were carried out at least as far back as the Neolithic period, before 3000 B.C. By the prehistoric Iron Age, after 600 B.C., these customs were common all over northern Europe.

The Kalkriese depression was a profoundly mystical environment for the Germans, even before their great military success. On the south side of the track was the forest on the slope of the Kalkriese Hill, and on the north side were the marshy lowlands that extended to the Great Bog. The setting was rich in sacred associations, and thus ideal for celebrations of ritual and religion. Perhaps its special ritual potential was a factor in its choice as the spot for the German attack, along with the natural advantages it offered the native warriors over their Roman adversaries.

Besides sacrificing some of the men from the opposing army, the victors had to offer up to their gods some of the weapons and other goods captured. Because of the immense significance of this battle victory, they offered objects in a variety of traditional ways. The depositing of valued objects into water was a common means of making offerings to deities, just as the depositing of human sacrificial victims was. In ceremonies that lasted much of the day and were accompanied by incantations to gods of war and nature, groups of Germans threw swords, scabbards, daggers, helmets, coins, and other objects into different parts of the marshland north of the track. From one grassy bank in the marsh, a man threw a precious silver scabbard. At another, a warrior let a leather sack full of silver coins sink into the dark water. These actions were repeated hundreds of times all across the marshy depression. By depositing objects in many different places throughout the marsh, they could sanctify an extensive locale. They could both please the deities and create a special holy place for all of the tribal peoples who had participated in and benefited from this great victory.

Creating a Battlefield Sanctuary

The Germans constructed yet another part of this immense sacred site, in addition to the forest groves sanctified by the sacrifice of Roman officers and the marshy pools made holy by the bloody bodies of Romans and the treasures thrown in. This third part of the sanctuary was the battlefield itself—the site of the heroic deeds and grand accomplishments of the German warriors. To celebrate and commemorate the success of this immensely important event, the Germans wanted to achieve several aims. First and foremost, they wanted to create a memorial that the gods of war would understand as a supreme offering to them. Second, they wanted to construct a place that celebrated their successful resistance to Rome. Third, Arminius and his most devoted followers wanted this monument to serve as a sign of his leadership, as a means of shoring up his position as commander for future political struggles among the German tribes.

That the Germans would leave the Roman dead in place was a foregone conclusion and a first decision toward creating the ritual site on the battlefield. They had no interest in performing funerary ceremonies for the enemy soldiers anyway, and their decaying bodies and bleaching bones would starkly mark the site as the place of the great victory over the Roman legions. In addition, the Germans left some special objects on the site, arranged on the part of the battlefield where the fighting had been most intense—in front of the sod wall. All along the wall, the concentration of Roman bodies and body parts was especially dense. Many mules and horses lay along the wall as well, still wearing their ornamental harnesses, yokes, and bronze bells (see illustration 28).

One of the special objects placed on the edge of the killing zone by the wall was a mask helmet made of iron (illustration 29). Consisting of an iron face with openings for eyes, nostrils, and mouth, it had belonged to an auxiliary cavalryman who was serving with Varus's troops. The object had been specially crafted for him, and, though somewhat stylized, it represented his own facial features. He wore it not in battle but on ceremonial occasions, such as parades and display drills. He had been carrying this treasured possession on his saddle, and in the battle it had come loose and fallen off. A German scavenging the battlefield picked it up. Instead of throwing it into one of the black pools in the marsh, the Germans decided to place this special piece next to the sod wall. They valued it highly as a sign of their victory, because it was an unusual trophy, different from any of the equipment that German soldiers carried or wore. It was almost a portrait of one of their defeated enemies. But before placing it on the site, one of the Germans cut off the sheet of silver that covered the face. Silver was precious and always needed for making ornaments, and the significance of the face mask would not be lessened by removing this second metal.

Remembrance, Visitation, and Transformation

In the following days and weeks, many people came from nearby communities and from farther away to visit the site and pay homage to the Germans who had planned so carefully and fought so hard to defeat these Roman legions. Given their past experiences with the Romans, they expected reprisals, but they nonetheless felt that they had succeeded in delivering a resounding blow to the imperial army and hoped that their victory would have a long-lasting impact in discouraging Rome from continuing its attempts to conquer their lands.

During the next few years, groups of Germans continued to come regularly to the site to pay their respects, to celebrate their peoples' victory, and to express thanks to the war gods who had favored their efforts in the ambush.

Meanwhile, already in the months following the battle, the mammals, birds, insects, and bacteria had reduced the thousands of corpses to bones. What had been the well-worn track around the Kalkriese Hill took on a different appearance. Weeds and wildflowers sprang up everywhere, richly fertilized by the copious blood that had soaked into the ground, but the dominant aspect of the place was tens of thousands of bones, some bleached by the sun, lying on the surface.

Desecration by the Romans

Six years after the battle, during the Romans' final, fruitless attempts to defeat these resistant peoples, the general Germanicus and his troops visited the battle site. When they came upon the huge mass of whitened bones and the weapons that had been left in place or purposely arranged by the Germans when they created their sanctuary, they felt outrage at the disrespectful treatment of their fallen comrades, whose bones lay exposed and uncared for in the open air.

They began to bury the bones out of respect for their dead comrades, unaware that they were destroying a sacred site of the Germans (not that they would have cared even if they had known). The number of bones on the site was enormous and the task overwhelming. Some soldiers dug pits in the ground and placed bones in the holes, covering them with the fresh soil. Sometimes they picked up nearby weapons and deposited them in the pits as well, as signs of the efforts the dead men had made in the battle. A number of legionaries gathered up large quantities of bones and heaped them into great piles. They then covered them with great mounds of earth. But Germanicus did not want to keep his men for very long on this task, and after half a day he ordered the burial work to stop and his troops to leave the site and undertake the job of conquering the Germans once and for all. They had made hardly a dent in the huge mass of bones covering the ground along the track, but they had succeeded in giving at least some of their countrymen burial, removing their bones from exposure on the surface and sheltering them in the security of the earth.

Reconsecration of the Sanctuary

From the woods beyond the eroding sod wall, some Germans watched the Roman legionaries as they moved bones and weapons on the sacred site. For them, those actions were a sacrilege, desecrating the sacred site that the victorious warriors had created. They told their comrades about what they had seen, and groups of Germans came to the site to undo what Germanicus's troops had done. They tore down the mounds the Romans had built, scattering the bones that lay underneath. Where they could identify freshly dug pits, they burrowed into the soft soil, ripping out bones and buried weapons, scattering them again over the surface of the battle site. Although it had been defiled temporarily by the Roman tampering, the place was once again restored to its sanctified status.

Forgetting and Remembering

The site remained sacred to the German peoples of the region for many years after the battle. No community established a settlement on this land, nor were cattle allowed to graze in the wet meadows. Many people made pilgrimages to the site, especially those who had lost sons, brothers, and fathers in the battle, as well as others who wished to honor the achievement of the warriors who had won the decisive victory that broke Rome's will to continue its attempts to expand eastward beyond the Rhine.

After several generations, people's links with the place gradually vanished. The Roman border had been firmly set at the lower Rhine, and there was no indication that Rome would attempt further military ventures eastward. In fact, the whole relationship between Rome and the Germans had changed. Many Germans now served as auxiliaries in the Roman bases on the Rhine, and many others had entered into contracts to produce food, iron tools, leather and textiles, and other goods for the tens of thousands of troops stationed along the Rhine and Danube frontiers. Thus the immediate significance of the battle site faded in the memory of most Germans.

But although visits to the sanctuary gradually declined and finally ceased a few generations after the battle, memory of the event remained active in stories and legends among the

Germanic tribes. In the succeeding centuries, few people had any idea where the battle had taken place, when it had happened, or who the leaders and tribal participants had been. But the memory of a great battle against the Romans, which the German warriors had won, lived on in stories, songs, and legends.

11

THE IMMEDIATE OUTCOME

The outcome of the battle had immediate and profound effects on Rome and its policies and on the tribal peoples of northern Europe. The effects on Rome are apparent in the historical documents. Those on the native peoples can be seen in the archaeological evidence of their burials, their settlements, and the objects they made and used.

Reaction in Rome

When news of the disaster arrived in Rome, brought by messengers from the Rhineland, the city was getting ready to celebrate Tiberius's victory in putting down the rebellions in Pannonia and Dalmatia. That task had taken him nearly three years, from A.D. 6 to 9, and had cost many Roman lives. The Senate had approved the celebration of a triumph, and preparations were well under way.

The first reaction of Augustus and his counselors to the news of the loss of the three legions was shock and fear. The regular reports that had been coming back to Rome over the past decade from the commanders on the Rhine had been positive, leading Augustus to believe that the peoples east of the Rhine were largely under Roman control. He had confidently appointed Varus commander of the Rhine legions to oversee the final pacification of Germany and its integration into the Roman provincial structure. Upon hearing of the disaster, Augustus immediately feared for the Rhineland bases and for the provinces of Gaul.

But Augustus's reaction to the news, and that of others in Rome, was not only alarm at the threatened geopolitical situation on the Rhine and in Gaul. Losing three out of its total twenty-eight legions was certainly a very serious blow to Rome, both logistically and psychologically, especially since Rome's military establishment was considered to be almost invincible. On another level, though, the report of the defeat of Varus's legions had a profound impact on the way Romans saw themselves and their place in the world. It told Romans that they were not invincible, despite their military successes of the past decades, and it rekindled the deep-seated and long-standing fears created by the earlier experiences with northern invaders—the Gauls in the early fourth century B.C. and the Cimbri and Teutones in the late second century. For this reason, the catastrophe in the northern forests represented an event even more alarming than the loss of the legions and of Roman political and military authority and control in Germany. In his discussion of Augustus's and Tiberius's reaction to word of the Varus disaster, Velleius Paterculus writes that the Germans "threatened Italy with a war like that of the Cimbri and Teutones."

Augustus immediately ordered guards posted in Rome to discourage any sympathetic uprisings among foreign residents of the city that might occur as a result of the news of the disaster. He dismissed his German cavalry guard, comprising soldiers from tribes allied with Rome, though those men had shown no signs of disloyalty, because he feared that some of them might turn against him in concert with their countrymen in the north. He granted greater powers to governors in the provinces to control the provincial populations, out of fear that word of the revolt in Germany might spur similar uprisings elsewhere. He vowed that he would sponsor games in honor of Jupiter as soon as matters had calmed down, an act that his predecessors had carried out following the successful defeat of the Cimbri and their allies in 101 B.C.

Augustus's biographer Suetonius writes that the emperor was so distressed by the disaster that he let his hair and beard grow for months afterward and would frequently call out, "Quinctilius Varus, give me back my legions!" In the following years, Augustus observed the anniversary of the defeat in mourning.

Augustus's Response

In order to stabilize what he feared was a precarious situation on the Rhine frontier, Augustus again sent Tiberius to take command of the legions there. Tiberius redistributed the Roman forces in the Rhineland and increased the defensive capabilities of the military bases. During the next few years he crossed the Rhine with some of his troops. According to Velleius Paterculus, he "penetrated into the heart of the country, opened up military roads, devastated fields, burned houses, routed those who came against him, and, without loss to the troops with which he had crossed, he returned, covered with glory, to winter quarters." Since Velleius was enamored of Tiberius and tended to exaggerate his accomplishments, we need to read these lines with a grain of salt. No archaeological traces of military roads from this period have been identified, nor have archaeologists detected any signs of the layers of charcoal that we might expect from widespread burning of settlements. Furthermore, it is difficult to imagine that, after Arminius's great victory in A.D. 9, Tiberius's legions could march through the landscape with no losses, particularly since the huge investment of troops a few years later resulted in no conclusive victories for the Romans.

Tiberius conducted campaigns across the Rhine in A.D. 11 and

12 against the Bructeri and the Marsi for the purpose of avenging the defeat of Varus and his legions, but those campaigns had
no great effect. Perhaps the campaigns were intended to "show
the flag" as much as anything else—to demonstrate to the
Germans that Rome still controlled the west bank of the Rhine
and that its forces could move freely in the lands to the east when
they chose to do so. In A.D. 13, Tiberius was granted power equal
to that of Augustus in Rome. When Augustus died, in the following year, Tiberius became emperor.

After Augustus's death, several statements left by him were read
in the Roman Senate, some of which have important bearing on
Rome's policies with respect to the Germans. One of these statements was his list of accomplishments, the *Res Gestae Divi Augusti*,
in which he asserts that he oversaw the conquest of lands to the
mouth of the Elbe, but makes no reference at all to the Varus disaster. Is it possible that he still misunderstood the situation east of
the Rhine, even after the loss of the three legions? Could he have
thought that Rome was in control of the lands between the
Rhine and the Elbe? Or was he simply exaggerating the extent of
Rome's activities beyond the Rhine frontier and choosing to
omit the profound embarrassment of the Varus catastrophe?

Some Roman writers, including Tacitus and Cassius Dio,
mention a statement left by Augustus ordering that the Empire
not be expanded further after his death. But some modern scholars doubt whether such a document ever existed, arguing that
the idea of not expanding the Empire any further was Tiberius's,
not Augustus's. With decades of experience fighting on the frontiers, Tiberius felt that the costs involved in conquering and
administering new territories, ever farther from Rome and against
increasingly resistant enemies, outweighed the possible benefits.
Tiberius may have found it politically expedient to tell the
Senate that Augustus had advised him against further expansion.
In any case, there is compelling historical evidence that plans for
imperial expansion were rapidly winding down.

Rome's Last Campaigns against Arminius: Germanicus in A.D. 14–16

In A.D. 13, the year before his death, Augustus dispatched Germanicus, the son of Drusus, to take command of the legions on the Rhine. Tiberius remained in Rome to aid Augustus in the administration of the Empire. By this time, the redeployment of troops overseen by Tiberius had resulted in a total of eight legions stationed on the Rhine frontier. Four were in lower Germany—the 5th and 21st Legions at Xanten and the 1st and 20th at or near Cologne. Four were in upper Germany—the 2nd, 12th, 14th, and 26th. This deployment, about one-third of Rome's entire military force, represented a huge concentration of troops on the Rhine.

Between A.D. 14 and 16, Germanicus led a series of major campaigns across the Rhine into German territory, where the Roman legions again confronted Arminius and his allies. Tacitus informs us that the purpose of those campaigns was to avenge the Varus defeat, not to expand the Empire, and most modern investigators seem to agree in essence with that assessment. Certainly the several major battles and the more numerous small skirmishes did not alter the frontier situation that had resulted from Arminius's victory in A.D. 9. At some point in the year 15, Segestes, who had been held prisoner by Arminius's forces, was able to send word to Germanicus for help. Germanicus's troops released Segestes and took Thusnelda (Arminius's wife and Segestes's daughter, who was pregnant) into Roman captivity.

In A.D. 15, the Roman army under Germanicus and Arminius's German warriors met in two major confrontations, neither of which was decisive. Germanicus directed a land and water offensive, with troops marching from the Rhineland bases eastward and others sailing up the Ems River from the North Sea in order to attack the Cherusci and the Bructeri. During the course of this summer campaign, Germanicus and some of his men visited the battle site where Varus and his three legions were defeated. Somewhere in the boggy lowlands around the Ems at a location Tacitus calls the *pontes longi* (long causeways), Arminius's troops attacked the Roman army, and the fighting lasted over two days. The Roman preoccupation with the Varus defeat is reflected in Tacitus's description of a dream that came to Caecina, one of Germanicus's generals: "the general's night was disturbed by a sinister and alarming dream: for he imagined that he saw Quintilius Varus risen, blood-bedraggled, from the marsh, and heard him calling." But in this battle the sides were evenly matched, and neither won a decisive victory.

The final major Roman campaign against Arminius and his allies came in A.D. 16. Germanicus commanded eight legions, along with auxiliary units, overland from the Rhine, up the Ems River, and perhaps up the Weser as well, and met the enemy on a plain that Tacitus called Idistaviso, a place somewhere near the Weser River that has not yet been identified archaeologically. One event recounted by Tacitus is of particular interest regarding Roman ideas about Arminius and other Germans. The Roman army approached the Weser from the west; Arminius and his troops, from the east. Among the Roman forces was Flavus, Arminius's brother. The two siblings shouted across the river to each other in an exchange that Tacitus uses to represent the two opposing positions among the Germans—those in favor of alliance with Rome and those against it.

Flavus insisted on "Roman greatness, the power of the [emperor] . . . the mercy always waiting for him who submitted himself. . . ." His brother [Arminius] urged "the sacred call of their country; their ancestral liberty; the gods of their German hearths; and their mother, who prayed, with himself, that he would not choose the title of renegade and traitor to his kindred . . . to the whole of his race in fact, before that of their liberator."

Flavus became so enraged that he prepared to collect his weapons and mount his horse to cross the river to fight his brother. But the Roman general Stertinius stopped him. Arminius all the while taunted Flavus from the other bank, partly in their native tongue and "much in Latin, as he had seen service in the Roman camp as a captain of native auxiliaries."

According to Tacitus, the result of the ensuing battle on the Weser was a Roman victory: "the enemy were slaughtered from the fifth hour of daylight to nightfall, and for ten miles the ground was littered with corpses and weapons." Shortly after this battle, the sides met again, now downstream on the Weser, at a place Tacitus called the Angrivarii wall. Again, according to Tacitus, the Roman side won, but the victory was indecisive. Germanicus sent some of the legions back toward the Rhine bases by land, but most took what was expected to be the quicker route, on shipboard down the Ems to the North Sea and from there to the Rhine. As they reached the sea, a storm struck, resulting in the sinking of numerous ships and the loss of many men and horses.

Tacitus's accounts of the Roman victories in the campaigns of A.D. 15 and 16 must be read with caution and with skepticism, because in the next year, Tiberius decided to give up the attempt to subdue the Germans and recalled Germanicus to Rome. The reason for these decisions must have lain in the Germans' tough resistance. Even with the enormous strength of eight legions, Germanicus and his army were unable to thwart the indigenous peoples' military resistance. A variety of factors aided the Germans in their struggles. The effort Rome expended on the campaigns was vastly out of proportion to any conceivable gain from acquiring this new territory. As many texts, including those by Tacitus, indicate, the Romans regarded Germany as a wild territory of endless forests and forbidding swamps, without the wealth of resources that Gaul had to offer. Tiberius may have felt that Roman military efforts would be better applied in the eastern parts of the Empire, where greater wealth was available to be extracted for the imperial coffers. On the eastern frontiers, there were also threats, especially from the Parthians, that required attention.

However Tiberius weighed these different considerations, it is clear that Arminius's defeat of Varus and his legions in A.D. 9 played a decisive role. That event forced Rome to recognize the challenges it faced if it persisted in its expansionary policy east of the Rhine. At the same time, it gave the Germanic groups confidence that they could withstand the onslaught of the Roman legions. With Tiberius's decision in A.D. 17 to discontinue the Roman campaigns across the lower Rhine, the Rhine River again became the border between the Roman world and the Germanic peoples, as it had been established by Julius Caesar. For the next four centuries of their presence in Europe north of the Alps, the Romans, in dealing with the peoples east of the Rhine, had to rely on diplomacy, not military might.

The Death of Arminius

The historical sources tell us that the German victory over Varus and the Roman legions won great honors and prestige for Arminius as the leader of the attack, both among the Cherusci and among neighboring peoples. As a tribe, the Cherusci gained in reputation as the leading ally in the confrontation. Apparently as a result of this great military success of Arminius and his people, new tribes joined the coalition, including the Semnoni and Langobardi, both of whom had been allied with Maroboduus. The growing rivalry between Arminius and Maroboduus as the two most powerful leaders of native peoples east of the Rhine frontier led to a battle between their forces in A.D. 17. The results were not immediately decisive, but Arminius emerged with expanded power.

As Arminius's political position grew, disagreements between the different factions within the Cherusci intensified. Arminius's rivals accused him of trying to become a king. In the turmoil, some of his formerly loyal followers, including Arminius's own uncle Inguiomerus, left him and allied themselves with Maroboduus.

According to Tacitus, in the year 19, a chief of the Chatti tribe proposed to the Roman Senate that he kill Arminius with poison. The reply recorded by Tacitus was that "it was not by treason nor in the dark but openly and in arms that the Roman people took vengeance on their foes." Two years later, Arminius was killed by members of his own people, the Cherusci. All we know about the circumstances of his death comes from Tacitus.

> Arminius . . . began to aim at kingship, and found himself in conflict with the independent temper of his countrymen. He was attacked by arms, and, while defending himself with chequered results, fell by the treachery of his relatives.

As a memorial honoring this tremendously successful enemy of Rome, Tacitus writes,

> Undoubtedly the liberator of Germany; a man who, not in its infancy as captains and kings before him, but in the high noon of its sovereignty, threw down the challenge to the Roman nation, in battle with ambiguous results, in war without defeat . . . he . . . receives less than his due from us of Rome. . . .

The End of Roman Occupation East of the Lower Rhine

The defeat of the Roman legions under Varus in A.D. 9 meant the end of Roman occupation in the lands east of the lower Rhine.

The last of the Roman bases on the Lippe, at Haltern and Oberaden, were abandoned, never to be reoccupied. Traces of small forts that may have been built during the campaigns of Germanicus have been identified beyond the Lippe, for example at the Sparrenburger Egge, near Bielefeld, but they represent no more than temporary outposts used only during the summer campaigns. The civic center at Waldgirmes, in the Taunus, and the associated base at Dorlar were also given up for good in A.D. 9. Never again, during the succeeding four centuries of intensive Roman activity in the Rhineland, would the Roman military attempt to establish a foothold east of the lower Rhine.

During the occupation of Haltern, Oberaden, Waldgirmes, and the other forward points east of the Rhine, the Roman soldiers often had close contacts with the local peoples. Goods were bought and sold between them, and soldiers and natives got to know one another. The end of those interactions had implications for local economies, which had benefited from the business from the larger numbers of troops stationed at the bases, and also for the images that people developed about one another. The subsequent decades saw regular interactions between the Roman bases on the west bank of the Rhine and native groups on the east, but these interactions were different in significant ways from the earlier ones.

Impact on European Society

Unlike Haltern and Oberaden, whose abandonment is well dated, the sites of the native peoples have not left evidence of abrupt changes that happened in A.D. 9. Instead, we can identify gradual processes of change, in the context of which we can understand the success of Arminius's attack on the Roman legions and which were in turn strengthened by that success. Above I discussed the spread of the new practice of weapon burial and showed how this development illustrates the increasingly militarized way of life and attitudes of the peoples east of the Rhine as they prepared themselves, organizationally and psychologically, for their showdown with Rome.

During the first half of the first century A.D.—before and after the year 9—the number of weapon graves increased, and the amount of wealth buried in these graves increased, in many regions. A considerable number of graves were outfitted with complete sets of weapons—sword, lance, and shield—while the majority still contained only lance and shield. Many of the graves with full weaponry also contained ornate fibulae—decorative clothing clasps, usually of bronze or iron—and Roman bronze vessels, sometimes serving as the urn containing cremated remains. Silver came to play an increasingly important role in expressing status and wealth in these graves. Fibulae were often of silver, and silver was employed as trim on swords, scabbards, and drinking vessels. Earlier, silver had been rare in these societies, and its use now for decorative trim resulted from their borrowing the idea from Roman officers' equipment. Probably some of the silver used to cast the fibulae and make the ornamental attachments for weapons found in these graves was scavenged from the battlefield at Kalkriese. Some of the Roman bronze vessels used as urns may have had the same source.

This cemetery evidence can be interpreted to show that trends that were under way before A.D. 9—burial of weapons in some men's graves, increasing quantities of wealth in some— were reinforced by the outcome of the great battle. After the defeat of the Roman legions, military ideology came to play an even greater role in the societies east of the Rhine. Differences in social status increased, with the growth in power of the native societies in relation to Rome. The men who played leadership roles in the battle must have gained in status, and in wealth from booty collected. The great quantity of material won in the battle—the iron weapons and tools, silver and gold ornaments, bronze and silver vessels, and gold, silver, and bronze coins—may itself have had a major impact on social developments among the peoples involved, contributing to greater differentiation between individuals, depending upon the roles they played in the battle and the status they possessed before it. Changes in burial patterns throughout the regions east of the lower Rhine indicate that during the first half of the first century A.D. society became increasingly hierarchical.

Change is also apparent in settlements. Before the time of the battle, the characteristic settlement pattern throughout the North European Plain east of the lower Rhine consisted of single farmsteads or clusters of three or four farmsteads, such as the settlement at Meppen. During the first century A.D., a widespread change is apparent, with the growth of larger and more complex settlements, reflecting larger and socially more differentiated communities. Many of the new, larger settlements were enclosed by fences, and for the first time we can use the term "village" in reference to these sites. Well-documented examples are at Feddersen Wierde and Flögeln (see illustration 30), both in Lower Saxony. In each case, excavations have shown the growth of the settlements, from small hamlets of four or five houses and with outbuildings, to communities with many more structures. At Feddersen Wierde, social differences become clear within the community. Some houses were built better than others, and goods of higher quality have been found in the better-built houses than in the others.

An especially interesting example of changes in society and economy is at the settlement of Daseburg, just southeast of the upper Lippe River. Archaeologists excavated what appeared to be a typical small farming settlement established around A.D. 2.5. They found remains of a building that had served as both a house and a barn for livestock, a granary, several structures for keeping hay, cellar holes for food storage, and small sheds used for workshops. Among the crafts in evidence are spinning and weaving of textiles, and smelting of iron and forging of iron tools. But they also found remains of other, surprisingly complex craft activities. Two small structures with sunken floors situated to the northeast of the farm buildings contained abundant remains of bronze and ironworking. Elsewhere on the site was evidence for the processing of silver and lead as well. Partly made objects and scrap material indicate that the crafts workers at Daseburg made fibulae and other ornaments of silver, bronze, and iron.

The prominence of silver is striking here, because that metal does not occur to any appreciable extent on earlier settlements. Perhaps some of this metal, and some of the bronze, had its origin on the battlefield at Kalkriese. A particularly noteworthy feature of the small farming community of Daseburg is its participation in the production of specialized and highly valued ornaments. Surely the silver fibulae were destined not just for local use but also for exchange in the larger commercial networks that were expanding at this time.

At the present stage of analysis, we can only speculate that some of the silver and bronze in the cemeteries and settlements east of the Rhine came from objects plundered at Kalkriese. The ongoing changes in society and economy are clearly represented in sites all over the lands beyond of the Rhine frontier. The success of the local forces in that great battle, and the resultant expulsion of the Roman legions from the Lippe valley and effective end of their hopes for territorial conquest east of the lower Rhine, opened the way for the acceleration of social and economic changes that were already under way.

12
THE MEANING OF THE BATTLE

The Larger Impact

The *effects* of Arminius's defeat of the Roman legions in A.D. 9 have been enormous for European and world history. In this final chapter, I highlight some of these. I then close by reflecting on the importance of the distinction between the two fundamentally different ways of knowing about the past that I have explored in this book—history and archaeology. Written sources about events and the material remains of those events offer us two very different ways of understanding the past. The sources that are available to us, and those we choose to follow, determine how we think about that past.

After Tiberius called Germanicus back from Germany in A.D. 17 and ended Roman designs on the lands east of the lower Rhine, the Rhine became a highly fortified frontier of the Empire. The large number of troops stationed in the bases on the west bank of the river had a profound and long-lasting impact on local economies. The tens of thousands of men at Nijmegen, Xanten, Cologne, Bonn, Mainz, and other sites required vast quantities of grain, vegetables, meat, wine, and other foodstuffs. Most of these were produced in the vicinities of the bases by local farmers. Much of the weaponry, equipment, pottery, and personal ornamentation was manufactured in workshops in civilian settlements established near the bases. The Roman demand for goods created a huge surplus production in food and manufactured products, and thus greatly stimulated local economies. During the first and second centuries A.D., new cities were established at the sites of many of the bases, of which Cologne and Mainz became two of the largest and most important. At the time, the Rhineland was one of the most prosperous parts of the Roman Empire.

The Rhine remained the boundary between the Roman world and the unconquered lands to the east throughout the Roman period, into the fifth century A.D. When Christianity spread in parts of late Roman Europe, many of the important early centers were in the Rhineland, such as Bonn, Cologne, and Trier. The Rhineland thus remained a meeting zone of different cultures well into the medieval period, a point emphasized by R. W. Southern in his classic *The Making of the Middle Ages* (1959). Vestiges of this cultural frontier survive in the modern world. The boundary between countries that speak Romance languages— derived from Latin—and Germanic languages is the Rhineland. Peoples west of the Rhine are traditionally wine drinkers, while those east of the Rhine are traditionally beer drinkers.

I do not want to push this point too far, but one can reasonably argue that in stopping Roman designs on conquest east of the lower Rhine, the native warriors of A.D. 9 established a cultural, and sometimes political, boundary of very long duration.

Why the Romans Lost

Rome lost the Battle of the Teutoburg Forest, and three of its legions, because Augustus and his advisers did not understand the peoples of northern Europe or the changes those societies were undergoing.

Up to A.D. 9, Rome had won a long series of stunning military victories in Europe and elsewhere. It had suffered setbacks as well, but the official propaganda emphasized the successes. Indeed, Augustus made a great point of presenting to the people of Rome elaborate monuments, inscriptions, and coin images to glorify the Roman legions' successes. He downplayed the failures. In times before the creation of a free press and before the existence of diverse media not all controlled by the government, it was very difficult for the people of Rome to learn what was really going on. The sculpture and inscriptions with which Augustus adorned Rome glorified the achievements by the army. Augustan writers such as Livy and Virgil helped foster the public sense that Rome was destined to rule the world.

In addition to this general ideology of Rome's superiority over all neighbors, the prevailing attitude toward the peoples of northern Europe was to hold them in low regard. They were certainly not represented as foes capable of withstanding Roman power. From Caesar's first portrayals of the Germans as simple people with much smaller communities than the Gauls, there are no texts to indicate that Romans took them seriously as a military force. With the benefit of hindsight, of course, we can see many signs of their military prowess. Caesar hired German mercenaries precisely because of their effectiveness. In Cassius Dio's accounts of Drusus's campaigns into northern Germany, we read of occasions on which his enemies came close to trapping and severely defeating his army. But it is not clear how extensively this information was disseminated in Rome, or how seriously Augustus and his advisers took it. In the monumental architecture, the inscriptions, and the literature of the Augustan Age, there is no evidence that any officials in Rome were seriously concerned about a military threat in the north, despite the memories of the Gallic attack on Rome in 387 B.C. and the violent migrations of the Cimbri and Teutones.

Even the texts that deal directly with the Varus catastrophe describe the outcome as something other than a military victory for the Germans. The authors blame Varus for his carelessness, Arminius for his treachery, and the untamed environment and bad weather—never the capability of the local fighters relative to that of the Romans legions. Augustus blamed the defeat on Rome's failure to perform adequate rituals to gain favor with the gods. The Romans simply could not believe that their military forces had been outfought by the northern barbarians.

The archaeological evidence shows not only that the native peoples were vastly more capable technologically and organizationally than the Romans believed but also that they changed their military hardware, their attitudes toward the Roman intruders, and their economy during the decades before the battle of A.D. 9. Even Caesar's understanding of the peoples east of the Rhine in the middle of the final century B.C. was flawed. But from the time of Caesar on, the archaeology shows considerable change in increased production of weaponry, better-quality weapons, larger communities, and more highly developed communications between groups throughout the regions that Rome was trying to subdue.

These changes could have been evident to Rome. Large numbers of Roman imports indicate the existence of considerable interaction between the Roman world and the north. Merchants and other travelers could have reported their observations about changes in the Iron Age societies to officials in Rome. But all of the evidence in Rome suggests that Augustus and other Roman officials would not have been receptive to the information in such reports. Dieter Timpe and others have shown that Romans considered the barbarian peoples unchanging and unchangeable. Roman historical tradition emphasized continuity, not change. Indigenous peoples, especially, were regarded as immutable. This was the fatal flaw for the Romans. The world of northern Europe was changing, largely in response to processes set in motion by Rome's own actions in Gaul, but the Romans were largely oblivious to the changes.

Texts and Material Culture: History and Archaeology

In this book, we have considered two quite distinct ways of knowing about the past, in order to try to understand an event of signal importance in European and world history. One is through written texts; the other is through archaeological evidence. The texts were all written by Romans, or by Greeks who represented views closely linked to those of Rome, and they provide us not only with a view of the "facts" as the writers understood them but also with the writers' interpretations of why and how the great battle occurred. We have no texts written by their opponents, because at that time the peoples of northern Europe did not have a system of writing. To understand those peoples, we use the evidence of archaeology—the material remains left from their settlements, their cemeteries, and the objects that they made and used.

There are basic differences between text-based understandings of the past and archaeology-based ones. We belong to literate, text-oriented societies. From our earliest days in school, we are encouraged to read and to use written texts as sources of information. In examining the past, we tend to privilege written over material sources of information, because we have been trained to do so. I am constantly surprised in reading accounts of the Battle of the Teutoburg Forest, and of the developments leading up to it, to see how many investigators still take the Roman texts at face value, even though they are inconsistent. In most cases, modern writers adopt the version of events supplied by Cassius Dio, probably because his is the most detailed and colorful version, though it was written two centuries after the event and seems to contradict the versions of Tacitus and Florus. As I suggested in chapter 3, none of the accounts is reliable in detail, in the sense that we expect a modern newspaper account to get all the "facts" right. None of the authors was an eyewitness, and none of them explains where the writer got this information. The purpose of Roman historical writing was not to describe events in what we would consider accurate detail, but rather to make events understandable to their Roman readers in terms of their worldview. As the contemporary novelist Tim O'Brien has observed about understanding accounts of a war as recent as that in Vietnam, "In any war story, but especially a true one, it's difficult to separate what happened from what seemed to happen."

The texts by Velleius Paterculus, Tacitus, Florus, Cassius Dio, and the others provided their Roman readers with accounts that were meant to satisfy their desires for understanding what had happened east of the Rhine, but they were not aimed at our quite different expectations. We are troubled by the inconsistencies between the accounts, but the Roman reader perhaps was not. The important aspects for Roman readers were that the commander on the scene apparently failed miserably, that the Germanic ally whom the Romans had trusted proved treacherous, and that the miserable environment of the north aided the humans who inhabited it. And perhaps the failure to propitiate the gods with the proper rituals played a key role in the disaster.

By examining the archaeology, we can take a fundamentally different view of the developing situation, between 12 B.C., when the Roman campaigns into Germany began under Drusus, up to and including the battle and the events subsequent to it.

New Discoveries and New Perspectives

New texts from the Roman period are rarely discovered. The texts that form the basis of our historical understanding of the Battle of the Teutoburg Forest were found, translated, and published during the Renaissance, half a millennium ago (see chapter 2). But archaeological discoveries regularly add new information to what we know about the past. Just in the past couple of years, important new finds have come to light in the Lippe River valley. The marching camp at Holsterhausen has been known for some time, but in the course of recent construction work, four more marching camps have been found at the same location. Objects recovered place these sites in the time frame of the events discussed in this book. Among the finds mentioned in the initial reports are a helmet of a type represented at Kalkriese, a coin of a series that occurs there, and a section of a Roman road.

Together with these newly found Roman military camps, at this same site the excavations revealed a native settlement of more than forty buildings. Some contained both Roman-made and native-style objects. More than seventy furnaces for smelting iron show that this community specialized in producing iron, in quantities far beyond local needs. Perhaps this was a settlement like that at Daseburg, representing the economic changes that communities experienced in the years just after the native peoples drove the Roman legions from their lands.

What If the Romans Had Won?

"What if . . . ?" scenarios in history are in a sense pointless, but they can be fun, and they can help us appreciate the significance of an outcome. What would have happened if, as in the earlier situations under Drusus when the German warriors cornered the Roman legions, the Romans had extricated themselves or dealt the Germans a resounding defeat? Would the Romans have marched back to the Rhine bases, secure in the knowledge that they had taught the Germans a lesson and that the Germans would cease invading across the river? While some modern historians argue that this was the Roman goal in the eastern campaigns, the majority now believe that Rome was planning to establish a province between the Rhine and the Elbe. If the

Romans had defeated Arminius, perhaps they would have constructed bases on the west bank of the Elbe, similar to the ones they built along the Rhine. Would they have been content to stop there, or would later emperors have sought their own glory by conquering lands farther to the east? How would European history have been different if the Roman Empire had not been stopped at the Rhine?

APPENDIXES

1. How an Archaeological Site Is Formed

To understand the relationship between the Roman weapons and coins recovered at Kalkriese and the event that took place there in A.D. 9, we must consider how an archaeological site is formed (see map 9). An archaeological site does not reflect directly what happened at a place. Several transformations between an event and the recovery of material remains from that event by archaeologists alter the character of an archaeological deposit. Some of these transformations are cultural—caused by people—others are natural.

In the case of a battlefield, deposition of materials takes place when projectile weapons land on the ground, when fighters fall with their weapons and equipment, and when they drop their weapons and flee. After battles, the victors, or inhabitants of the surrounding countryside, typically collect everything that they see and can use from the field. The great majority of objects that fall to the ground during a battle never become buried to form part of an archaeological deposit.

Some objects are not collected by the survivors. Items deemed to be of no value are left on the surface. Bodies of combatants are likely to be consumed quickly by wild animals or slowly by bacteria. Organic materials such as textiles and wood decay. Iron and bronze left on the surface oxidize and disintegrate within a few years, depending upon the local chemical and moisture conditions. Small objects such as personal ornaments, buttons, and coins may be overlooked, particularly in high grass or in marshy environments. Some objects fall in hollows, in pits in the surface, and in streambeds where they are not readily visible. All such objects are likely to become buried through natural processes of deposition by wind, water, and vegetation, and thus become part of an archaeological deposit.

The important point is that the objects that archaeologists recover survive in the ground as a result of specific conditions of deposition and preservation. In order to interpret the meaning of archaeological finds recovered on a site, the archaeologist must understand those conditions and the transformations that the objects underwent between their use by living people and their discovery by archaeologists.

2. Roman Weapons Found at the Kalkriese Battle Site

In chapter 3, I noted briefly the character of Roman weapons that have been recovered at Kalkriese. Here I present more detail about some of them.

Most of the weapons that were used in hand-to-hand combat are represented by remains of typical iron blades and bronze attachments or trim. But one set of scabbard parts stands out as exceptional. About one and a quarter mile northwest of the Oberesch were found parts of a sword scabbard and of a sword belt, all made of silver. They include three clamps that held the two sides of the scabbard in place, all three with settings that held gems, in one case a carved garnet. Other silver pieces were a chape, attaching to the base of the scabbard, and a decorative disk. The owner of this silver-bearing weapon was surely a Roman officer, probably a centurion.

Among defensive weapons, in addition to those mentioned in chapter 3, are hooks used to attach chain mail, pieces of armor plate, buckles, and hinges from articulated armor. Metal parts of shields include typical iron and bronze elements, and also silver and gold trim, indicating officer rank. Parts of military belt hooks and belt attachments include objects made of bronze, some of them silver plated, and some objects of solid silver.

Many of the boots, represented by large numbers of iron nails, were left lying on the battlefield by the plunderers, because neither the shoes nor the iron in the nails was worth the trouble to recover. At one spot near the sod wall, the excavators found the forms of three boot soles, with nails still in place (about 120 per boot). These boot remains probably mark the exact spot where two soldiers fell.

Personal ornaments associated with the Roman legionaries include about one hundred fibulae, decorative pins worn on the shoulder to hold garments together. Most are bronze, but some are iron. Several iron finger rings hold inset gems.

Horses and mules—the cavalry mounts and the draft animals of the legions—are represented both by their bones (see chapter 3) and by metal objects that formed parts of their harnesses. Iron rings, bronze pendants (some decorated with silver), and iron spurs were standard components of cavalry equipment. Bronze rein fittings and attachments for yokes served as parts of the traction system for the mules that pulled the baggage wagons.

3. Museums, Roman Remains, and Archaeological Parks

A number of museums in Germany have excellent displays of materials pertaining to the subject of this book. All have websites that give their hours and tell about special exhibitions, often in

English as well as German, and some have maps showing how to find them. The Museum and Park Kalkriese,Venner Strasse 69, Bramsche, is situated on the battle site. The museum displays many of the objects recovered through excavation on the site and the park provides visitors with a good idea of what the area was like in A.D. 9.

Especially good displays of Roman material, both military and civilian, are at the following museums:

Rheinisches Landesmuseum, Colmantstrasse 14-16, Bonn

Westfälisches Römermuseum Haltern, Weseler Strasse 100, Haltern

Römisch-Germanisches Museum, Roncalliplatz 4, Köln (Cologne)

Landesmuseum Mainz, Grosse Bleiche 49-51, Mainz

Rheinisches Landesmuseum, Weimarer Allee 1, Trier

Regionalmuseum Xanten, Kapitel 18, Xanten

In the cities of Köln (Cologne), Mainz, and Trier, extensive stone and brick structures of the Roman period are still visible. Many guidebooks provide maps and descriptions of the Roman remains. Just outside the small city of Xanten is an extensive archaeological park with reconstructed buildings, workshops, Roman-style restaurants, and demonstrations (Archäologischer Park Xanten, Wardter Strasse, Am Amphitheater, Xanten).

Displays of material from settlements, cemeteries, and ritual deposits of the early Germans from around the time of the battle are in these museums:

Helms-Museum, Hamburger Museum für Archäologie und die Geschichte Harburgs, Museumsplatz 2, Hamburg

Niedersächsisches Landesmuseum Hannover, Willy-Brandt-Allee 5, Hannover

Archäologisches Landesmuseum, Schloss Gottorf, Schleswig

Related materials can be seen at museums in Denmark, especially the following:

Forhistorisk Museum Moesgård, Moesgård Alle 20, Århus

National Museum, Ny Vestergade 10, Copenhagen

Haderslev Museum, Dalgade 7, Haderslev

SOURCES
AND SUGGESTIONS FOR
FURTHER READING

Note: Frequently cited sources are abbreviated. The full references appear at the end.

PREFACE

Useful discussions of the experience of combat, medieval and modern, are J. Keegan, *The Face of Battle* (London, 1976), and P. Fussell, *Doing Battle* (Boston, 1996). On the origins and character of the Roman troops who served in northern Europe and on the peoples whom the Romans called Germans, see P. S. Wells, *The Barbarians Speak: How the Conquered Peoples Shaped Roman Europe* (Princeton, 1999).

1: AMBUSHED!

We do not know the details of exactly how Arminius's men attacked the Romans. In this first chapter, I use what we do know about the environment in which the battle took place, on the basis of the recent archaeological, geological, and paleobotanical research at Kalkriese, and about the equipment and marching order of the Roman army at the time (see chapter 7) to suggest what may have happened on that September day in A.D. 9. For reconstruction of the natural environment on and around the battle site, see W. Schlüter, "Die archäologischen Untersuchungen in der Kalkrieser-Niewedder Senke," in Schlüter, *Kalkriese*, pp. 13–51, and U. Dieckmann and R. Pott, "Archäobotanische Untersuchungen in der Kalkrieser-Niewedder Senke," ibid., pp. 81–105. A more general overview of landscape and vegetation in Europe during this period is H. Küster, *Geschichte der Landschaft in Mitteleuropa* (Munich, 1995). I use "about 18,000" men for the size of Varus's army. Estimates range from 15,000 to well over 20,000. As we see in chapter 3, different Roman accounts offer quite different versions of the circumstances of the battle. The reconstruction I offer here is based on my assessment of the evidence that is emerging from the archaeological investigations. Cassius Dio's description includes a severe storm that strikes just before the attack, but I suspect that this may be an embellishment added by that author (writing two hundred years after the battle) to dramatize the plight of the unlucky legions in what the Greek and Roman writers regarded as a forbidding landscape. Cassius Dio's account describes the battle as raging over three days. I see no reason to think that it lasted more than a single day and reconstruct it accordingly.

2: CREATION OF THE LEGEND

The discovery of the ancient Roman texts is recounted in L. D. Reynolds and N. G. Wilson, *Scribes and Scholars: A Guide to the Transmission of Greek and Latin Literature* (Oxford, 1968), L. D. Reynolds, *Texts and Transmission: A Survey of the Latin Classics* (Oxford, 1983), and H. Kloft, "Die Idee einer deutschen Nation zu Beginn der frühen Neuzeit," in Wiegels and Woesler, *Arminius*, pp. 197–210. On the ways the Arminius story was used from the sixteenth to the twentieth century, see H. Buck, "Der literarische Arminius: Inszenierungen einer sagenhaften Gestalt," in Schlüter, *Kalkriese*, pp. 267–81, V. Losemann, "'Varuskatastrophe' und 'Befreiungstat des Arminius': Die Germanienpolitik des Augustus in antiker und moderner Sicht," in Fansa, *Varusschlacht*, pp. 25–44, T. Kaufmann, "Edler Wilder, grausiger Heide, Fürstenknecht und Kämpfer für die Nation: Der Germane in den Bildprojektionen von der Bauernkriegszeit bis zur Romantik," ibid., pp. 45–70, H. C. Seeba, "Schwerterhebung: Zur Topographie des heroischen Subjekts (Grabbe, Kleist und Bandel)," ibid., pp. 71–86, and D. Timpe, "Die Schlacht im Teutoburger Wald: Geschichte, Tradition, Mythos," in Schlüter and Wiegels, *Rom*, pp. 717–37. Martin Luther's reference to Arminius: *Luther's Works*, vol. 13, *Selected Psalms II*, ed. by J. Pelikan (St. Louis, 1956), p. 59. Modern organizations in the United States identified with Hermann can be found on the Internet under "Herman." Role of Hermann in school curricula in modern Germany: R. Jooss, "Adam, Arminius und Hermann in der Schule," in K. Fuchs et al., eds., *Die Alamannen* (Stuttgart, 1997), pp. 31–36.

3: HISTORY AND ARCHAEOLOGY OF THE BATTLE

Most of the quotations from Roman and Greek sources come from the English translations of the classical works published in the Loeb Classical Library by Harvard University Press (see references below). The information I cite comes from the following sources: Ovid, *Tristia* 3.12.45–48 and 4.2.31–36; Manilius, *Astronomica* 1.898–900; and Strabo 7.1.4. Descriptions of the battle are in Velleius Paterculus 2.117–20; Cassius Dio 56.18–24; and Florus 2.30. For Tacitus on Germanicus's visit to battle site, see *Annals* 1.57–62.

Important discussions of these sources relative to the battle are E. Sander, "Zur Varusschlacht," *Archiv für Kulturgeschichte* 38 (1956): 129–51, W. John, "P. Quinctilius Varus" (see chapter 5), and R. Wiegels, "Kalkriese und die literarische Überlieferung zur *clades Variana*," in Schlüter and Wiegels, *Rom*, pp. 637–74.

Mommsen's *Die Örtlichkeit der Varusschlacht*, in which he correctly identified the battle site on the basis of analysis of the coin finds, was published in Berlin in 1885. F. Berger, *Kalkriese 1: Die römischen Fundmünzen* (Mainz, 1996), pp. 1–10, reports on the early coin finds. Tony Clunn describes his discovery of the coin hoard in the summer of 1987 and his subsequent finds in *In Quest of the Lost Legions* (London, 1999). Detailed descriptions of the environment at Kalkriese and of the excavations are W. Schlüter, "Die archäologischen Untersuchungen in der Kalkrieser-Niewedder Senke," in Schlüter, *Kalkriese*, pp. 13–51, and W. Schlüter, "Zum Stand der archäologischen Erforschung der Kalkrieser-Niewedder Senke," in Schlüter and Wiegels, *Rom*, pp. 13–60, and "The Battle of the Teutoburg Forest," in J. D. Creighton and R. J. A. Wilson, eds., *Roman Germany* (Portsmouth, R.I., 1999), pp. 125–59. The Roman finds from the site are well presented in G. Franzius, "Die römischen Funde aus Kalkriese," in Schlüter, *Kalkriese*, pp. 107–97, and in the issues of the journal *Varus-Kurier*. Human and animal bones are presented in S. Wilbers-Rost, "Die Ausgrabungen auf dem 'Oberesch' in Kalkriese," in Schlüter and Wiegels, *Rom*, pp. 61–89, H.-P. and M. Uerpmann, "Maultiere in der römischen Armee zur Zeit der Eroberungsfeldzüge in Germanien," in *Beiträge zur Archäozoologie und Prähistorischen Anthropologie* (Stuttgart, 1994), pp. 353–57, and in the *Varus-Kurier*. A website at www.kalkriese-varusschlacht.de provides the latest information about the ongoing excavations.

4: AUGUSTUS: ROME'S FIRST EMPEROR

Good sources on everyday life in Rome at the time of the battle are T. Cornell and J. Matthews, *Atlas of the Roman World* (New York, 1982), S. James, *Ancient Rome* (London, 1990), L. Adkins and R. A. Adkins, *Handbook to Life in Ancient Rome* (New York, 1994), and P. Connolly, *The Ancient City: Life in Classical Athens and Rome* (Oxford, 1998). Augustus's impact on the city: N. Purcell, "Rome and Its Development under Augustus and His Successors," *CAH* 2, pp. 782–811.

On Augustus, Suetonius's biography is an important primary source, published in very readable form in Gaius Suetonius Tranquillus, *The Twelve Caesars*, trans. R. Graves, rev. ed. (New York, 1980). The modern biographies by A. H. M. Jones, *Augustus* (London, 1970), P. Southern, *Augustus* (London, 1998), and D. Kienast, *Augustus*, 3rd ed. (Darmstadt, 1999), are especially useful. Other important sources on Augustus's rise to power, the politics of his time, and Rome's expansion include R. Syme, *The Roman Revolution* (Oxford, 1952) and *The Augustan Aristocracy* (Oxford, 1986), *Kaiser Augustus und die verlorene Republik* (Berlin, 1988), P. Zanker, *The Power of Images in the Age of Augustus* (Ann Arbor, 1988), A. L. Kuttner, *Dynasty and Empire in the Age of Augustus* (Berkeley, 1995), J. A. Crook, "Augustus: Power, Authority, Achievement," *CAH* 2, pp. 113–46, E. S. Gruen, "The Expansion of the Empire under Augustus," *CAH* 2, pp. 147–97, and C. Pelling, "The Triumviral Period," *CAH* 2, pp. 1–69. Augustus's official statement of his accomplishments is conveniently presented in P. A. Brunt and J. M. Moore, *Res Gestae Divi Augusti: The Achievements of the Divine Augustus* (Oxford, 1967).

On Cleopatra and her relationships with Caesar and Antony, see W. W. Tarn, "The Triumvirs," in *CAH*, pp. 31–66, W. W. Tarn and M. P. Charlesworth, "The War of the East against the West," in *CAH*, pp. 66–111, and A. Meadows, "Sins of the Fathers: The Inheritance of Cleopatra, Last Queen of Egypt," in S. Walker and P. Higgs, eds., *Cleopatra of Egypt* (London, 2001), pp. 14–31. On Julia, see E. F. Leon, "Scribonia and Her Daughters," *Transactions and Proceedings of the American Philological Association* 82 (1951): 168–75, E. Miese, *Untersuchungen zur Geschichte der Julisch-Claudischen Dynastie* (Munich, 1969), pp. 2–34, and the two works by R. Syme cited above. For Augustus's policy east of the lower Rhine, see C. M. Wells, *The German Policy of Augustus* (Oxford, 1972).

5: VARUS AND THE FRONTIER

The available biographical information for Varus is presented in E. M. Smallwood, *The Jews under Roman Rule* (Leiden, 1976), pp. 106–14, W. John, "P. Quinctilius Varus," in Pauly-Wissowa, vol. 47, cols. 907–84 (Stuttgart, 1963), and R. Syme, *The Augustan Aristocracy* (Oxford, 1986). Roman authors on Varus: Velleius, 117–18; Florus, 2.30; and Cassius Dio, 56.18.

On the coins with the special Varus stamp, see F. Berger, "Das Geld der römischen Soldaten," in Schlüter, *Kalkriese*, pp. 211–30.

The Roman frontier along the Rhine has been intensively investigated for more than a century, and a huge number of publications present the results. More general sources about the Roman army and the experiences of soldiers are R. W. Davies, "The Daily Life of the Roman Soldier," in H. Temporini, ed.,

Aufstieg und Niedergang der römischen Welt, vol. 2, pt. 1 (Berlin, 1974), pp. 299–338, and *Service in the Roman Army* (Edinburgh, 1989) (source [p. 34] of Tacitus quotation on p. 99), M. Junkelmann, *Die Legionen des Augustus* (Mainz, 1986), A. K. Goldsworthy, *The Roman Army at War, 100 BC–AD 200* (Oxford, 1996), and G. Webster, *The Roman Imperial Army*, 3rd ed. (Norman, Okla., 1998). More specific studies of the places mentioned are C. M. Wells, *The German Policy of Augustus* (Oxford, 1972), S. von Schnurbein, "Untersuchungen zur Geschichte der römischen Militäranlagen an der Lippe," *Bericht der Römisch-Germanischen Kommission* 62 (1981): 5–101, H. Schönberger, "Die römischen Truppenlager der frühen und mittleren Kaiserzeit zwischen Nordsee und Inn," ibid., 66 (1985): 321–497, T. Bechert and W. J. H. Willems, *Die römische Reichsgrenze zwischen Mosel und Nordseeküste* (Stuttgart, 1995), J.-S. Kühlborn, "Haltern," in *Reallexikon*, vol. 13 (1999), pp. 460–69, and P. S. Wells, *The Barbarians Speak: How the Conquered Peoples Shaped Roman Europe* (Princeton, 1999). The catalogue for the new museum at Haltern provides a well-illustrated summary about soldiers at that site: R. Asskamp and R. Wiechers, *Westfälisches Römermuseum Haltern* (Münster, 1996). On Roman ships in the Rhineland, see B. Pferdehirt, *Das Museum für antike Schiffahrt* (Mainz, 1995). Letters at Vindolanda: A. K. Bowman, *Life and Letters on the Roman Frontier* (London, 1994) (source [pp. 127, 140] of quotations on p. 100). Marcus Caelius gravestone: R. Busch, ed., *Rom an der Niederelbe* (Neumünster, 1995), pp. 156–57. The Döttenbichl excavations have not yet been fully published, but preliminary information is in W. Zanier, "Der Alpenfeldzug 15 v. Chr. und die Eroberung Vindelikiens," *Bayerische Vorgeschichtsblätter* 64 (1999): 99–132. Dangstetten: R. Wiegels, "Zwei Bleimarken aus dem frührömischen Truppenlager Dangstetten," *Fundberichte aus Baden-Württemberg* 14 (1989): 427–56, and G. Fingerlin, *Dangstetten II* (Stuttgart, 1998). Ingot at Haltern: S. von Schnurbein, "Ein Bleibarren der 19. Legion aus dem Hauptlager von Haltern," *Germania* 49 (1971): 132–36. A very well-illustrated exhibition catalogue with many valuable articles about the frontier, relations between Romans and natives, and life in the newly established Roman towns is L. Wamser, ed., *Die Römer zwischen Alpen und Nordmeer* (Mainz, 2000).

6: ARMINIUS: THE NATIVE HERO

Since Arminius belonged to a society that did not have a system of writing, everything we know about him comes from Roman written sources and from extrapolations that we need to make from those sources and what we know about the archaeology of the period. Roman authors on Arminius: Velleius, 2.118; and Tacitus, *Annals* 1.55–68, 2.9–17, 44–46, 88. Discussions of Arminius as he was portrayed by the Roman writers include H. Callies, "Arminius: Historisches," *Reallexikon*, vol. 1 (1973), pp. 417–20, P. von Rohden, "Arminius," in Pauly-Wissowa, vol. 2 (1895), cols. 1190–200, H. Beck, "Arminius: Namenkundliches," in *Reallexikon*, vol. 1 (1973), p. 420, H. von Petrikovits, "Arminius," *Bonner Jahrbücher* 166 (1965): 175–93, D. Timpe, *Arminius-Studien* (Heidelberg, 1970), S. L. Dyson, "Native Revolts in the Roman Empire," *Historia* 20 (1971): 253–58, and W. Pohl, *Die Germanen* (Munich, 2000), pp. 93–96. On the war in Pannonia: A. Mócsy, *Pannonia and Upper Moesia* (Boston, 1974). Cherusci tribe: R. Wenskus, "Cherusker," in *Reallexikon*, vol. 4 (1981), pp. 430–35 and W. Will, "Römische 'Klientel-Randstaaten' am Rhein?" *Bonner Jahrbücher* 187 (1987): 44–55.

Many modern historians think that Arminius probably served as a commander of auxiliary troops in the war in Pannonia, but we do not know this for certain.

Much has been written about the conflicts between Romans and native peoples along and beyond the Rhine and Danube Rivers, some of which has been cited already. Other important accounts include R. Syme, "The Northern Frontiers under Augustus," in *CAH*, pp. 340–81, D. Timpe, "Rom und die Barbaren des Nordens," in M. Schuster, ed., *Die Begegnung mit dem Fremden* (Stuttgart, 1996), pp. 34–50, and R. Wolters, *Die Römer in Germanien* (Munich, 2000).

For the archaeology of the native peoples whom the Romans called "Germans," see B. Krüger, ed., *Die Germanen* (Berlin, 1988), M. Todd, *The Early Germans* (Oxford, 1992), and G. Kossack, *Dörfer im nördlichen Germanien vornehmlich aus der römischen Kaiserzeit* (Munich, 1997). On the historical sources: E. A. Thompson, *The Early Germans* (Oxford, 1965), H. Wolfram, *Die Germanen*, 2nd ed. (Munich, 1995). Settlement at Meppen: D. Zoller, "Eine Siedlung der vorrömischen Eisenzeit bei Meppen, Kr. Emsland," *Nachrichten aus Niedersachsens Urgeschichte* 46 (1977): 233–39. Health, life span, stature: B. Sellevold, U. L. Hansen, and J. B. Jørgensen, *Iron Age Man in Denmark* (Copenhagen, 1984).

Ockenhausen wooden trackway: M. Fansa and R. Schneider, "Die Bohlenwege bei Ockenhausen/Oltmannsfehn, Gde. Uplengen, Ldkr. Leer," *Archäologische Mitteilungen aus Nordwestdeutschland* 16 (1993): 23–43. Hodde: S. Hvass, *Hodde* (Copenhagen, 1985). Hjortspring: K. Randsborg, *Hjortspring* (Aarhus, 1995). Putsensen Grave 150: P. Roggenbuck, "Das Grab 150 von Putensen, Kr. Harburg," *Hammaburg* 6 (1983): 133–41. Military ideology: N. Roymans, "Romanisation and the Transformation of a Martial Elite-Ideology in a Frontier Province," in P. Brun, S. van der Leeuw, and C. R. Whitaker, eds., *Frontières d'empire: Nature et signification des frontières romaines* (Nemours, 1993), pp. 33–50. Germanic warrior bands: M. Hoeper and H. Steuer, "Zu germanischen 'Herresverbänden' bzw. 'Heerlagern' im Spiegel der Archäologie," in Schlüter and Wiegels, *Rom*, pp. 467–94.

7: WARFARE IN EARLY ROMAN EUROPE

Among the many valuable studies of the Roman army are R. Syme, "Some Notes on the Legions under Augustus," *Journal of Roman Studies* 23 (1933): 14–33, J. Roth, "The Size and Organization of the Roman Imperial Legion," *Historia* 43 (1994): 346–62, J. Warry, *Warfare in the Classical World* (Norman, Okla., 1995), L. Keppie, "The Army and the Navy," *CAH* 2, pp. 371–96, A. K. Goldsworthy, *The Roman Army at War, 100 BC–AD 200* (Oxford, 1996) and *Roman Warfare* (London, 2000), and P. Sabin, "The Face of Roman Battle," *Journal of Roman Studies* 90 (2000): 1–17. Important concerning the pictures of Roman legionary troops marching, fighting, and building is I. A. Richmond, *Trajan's Army on Trajan's Column* (London, 1982). M. C. Bishop and J. C. N. Coulson, *Roman Military Equipment* (London, 1993) is an excellent discussion of weaponry. Tacitus quotation on p. 134: *Annals* 1.51. On the sling, see W. B. Griffiths, "The Sling and Its Place in the Roman Imperial Army," in C. van Driel-Murray, ed., *Roman Military Equipment* (Oxford, 1989), pp. 255–79. On morale of the troops, see R. MacMullen, "The Legion as Society," *Historia* 33 (1984): 440–56, and A. D. Lee, "Morale and the Roman Experience in Battle," in A. B. Lloyd, ed., *Battle in Antiquity* (London, 1996), pp. 199–217.

Native German weaponry and warfare are treated in W. Adler, *Studien zur germanischen Bewaffnung* (Bonn, 1993), and K. Randsborg, *Hjortspring* (Aarhus, 1995). Vaedbro: F. Kaul, *Da våbnene tav* (Copenhagen, 1988). Recent summary of the Illerup find: J. Ilkjaer, "Illerup Ådal: Archäologisches," *Reallexikon*, vol. 15 (2000), pp. 347–53.

Roman military development: A. K. Goldsworthy, *Roman Warfare* (London, 2000). Rome's population: L. H. Ward, "Roman Population, Territory, Tribe, City, and Army Size from the Republic's Founding to the Veientane War, 509 B.C.–400 B.C.," *American Journal of Philology* 111 (1990): 5–39. Livy quotations, pp. 146, 147: 5.37, 42. An excellent, concise overview of Roman thought and action with regard to northern Europe is D. Timpe, "Entdeckungsgeschichte," in *Reallexikon*, vol. 7 (1989), pp. 337–89. A useful review of the written sources about the Cimbri and Teutones is H. Last, "The Cimbri and Teutoni," in *CAH*, 9:139–51 (Cambridge, 1932). Caesar's campaigns in Gaul: J. F. Drinkwater, *Roman Gaul* (Ithaca, N.Y., 1983), T. P. Wiseman, "Caesar, Pompey and Rome, 59–50 B.C.," in *CAH* 2, pp. 368–423, and K. Welch and A. Powell, eds., *Julius Caesar as Artful Reporter* (London, 1998). On Caesar's forays across the Rhine:

G. Walser, *Caesar und die Germanen* (Wiesbaden, 1956). Caesar's own account is translated in the Loeb Classical Library series as *The Gallic War* (Cambridge, Mass., 1986); quotation on p. 151: 6.21–22. An excellent discussion of the Rhine frontier from Caesar campaigns on is J. Kunow, "Die Militärgeschichte Niedergermaniens," in H. G. Horn, ed., *Die Römer in Nordrhein-Westfalen* (Stuttgart, 1987), pp. 27–109. Other valuable sources on the frontier and the campaigns of Drusus and Tiberius are R. Syme, "The Northern Frontier under Augustus," *CAH*, pp. 340–81, P. Moeller, "Drusus," in *Reallexikon*, vol. 6 (1986), pp. 204–15, and R. Wolters, *Römische Eroberung und Herrschaftsorganisation in Gallien und Germanien* (Bochum, 1990), "Germanien im Jahre 8 v. Chr.," in Schlüter and Wiegels, *Rom*, pp. 591–635, and *Die Römer in Germanien* (Munich, 2000). Inscription text, p. 150: L. Pauli, *Die Alpen in Frühzeit und Mittelatter* (Munich, 1980), p. 54. Cassius Dio quotation, p. 154: 54.33.

8: THE BATTLE

We do not know exactly what happened in the battle. In my interpretation of the texts, I side with Gerold Walser, Erich Sander, Walter John, and Dieter Timpe in believing that the details in the descriptions of the battle, including the character of the immediate surroundings in Cassius Dio, are not so much actual accounts of the specifics of the event as stereotypical representations based on motifs in Roman literature and general ideas about the peoples and the landscape of the region.

In composing this historical reconstruction, I have worked with what we know about Varus and the legions he commanded (chapter 5), Roman military tactics and weaponry (chapter 7), Roman accounts of the battle (chapter 3; see also R. Wiegels, "Kalkriese: Historisches," in *Reallexikon*, vol. 16 [2000], pp. 194–99), native German weaponry and tactics (chapter 7; also H. Steuer, "Kriegswesen," *Reallexikon*, vol. 17 [2001], pp. 336–73), the archaeological and topographical evidence at Kalkriese, and information from other, historically recorded battles.

Especially useful points of reference for trying to work out a likely scenario for the battle were J. Keegan's *The Face of Battle* (London, 1976), J. Warry's *Warfare in the Classical World* (Norman, Okla., 1995), V. D. Hanson's *The Soul of Battle* (New York, 1999) and *The Western Way of War* (Berkeley, 2000), and J. Carman's "Beyond the Western Way of War: Ancient Battlefields in Comparative Perspective," in J. Carman and A. Harding, eds., *Ancient Warfare* (Stroud, 1999), pp. 39–55.

A good recent discussion of iron production among the Germanic tribes at this time is H. Jöns, "Iron Production in Northern Germany," in C. Fabech and J. Ringtved, eds., *Settlement and Landscape* (Højbjerg, 1999), pp. 249–60.

9: THE HORROR: DEATH ON THE BATTLEFIELD

For trying to understand what happened to soldiers on the battlefield and in their suffering from wounds afterward, in addition to the sources cited above, B. Thordeman, *Armour from the Battle of Visby, 1361* (Stockholm, 1939), G. F. Linderman, *Embattled Courage: The Experience of Combat in the American Civil War* (New York, 1987), C. J. Arnold, "The Archaeology of Inter-Personal Violence," *Scottish Archaeological Review* 9 (1995): 71–79, and J. Carman, ed., *Material Harm: Archaeological Studies of War and Violence* (Glasgow, 1997), are especially helpful. R. A. Gabriel and K. S. Metz's *From Sumer to Rome: The Military Capabilities of Ancient Armies* (New York, 1991) is an excellent source of data on wounds inflicted by different kinds of weapons. On gladiatorial combat, see E. Köhne and C. Ewigleben, *Gladiators and Caesars: The Power of Spectacle in Ancient Rome* (London, 2000). In his writing on medicine, the Roman doctor Celsus describes how to treat specific kinds of battle wounds. For medical practice among the Germans of the period, see C. Daxelmüller, "Heilbräuche und Heilzauber," *Reallexikon*, vol. 14 (1999), pp. 161–64. The numbers involved are, of course, speculation.

10: THE VICTORS' CELEBRATIONS

This chapter is based on abundant archaeological evidence in northern Europe for the sacrifice and offering of human beings and of objects such as weapons and other valued items, and on Roman accounts of behaviors by victorious natives. Funerary rituals are described in B. Krüger, ed., *Die Germanen* (Berlin, 1988), and in M. Todd, *The Ancient Germans* (Oxford, 1992). On sacrifice of Roman captives, see the written accounts (chapter 3) and M. Green, *Dying for the Gods: Human Sacrifice in Iron Age and Roman Europe* (Stroud, 2001). Ritual significance of trees: H. Homann, "Baumkult," *Reallexikon*, vol. 2 (1976), pp. 107–10. Sanctuary created on the battlefield: C. von Carnap-Bornheim, "Archäologisch-historische Überlegungen zum Fundplatz Kalkrieser-Niewedder Senke in den Jahren zwischen 9 n. Chr. und 15 n. Chr.," in Schlüter and Wiegels, *Rom*, pp. 495–508. Ritual significance of mask helmets: G. Franzius, "Maskenhelme," ibid., pp. 117–48.

11: THE IMMEDIATE OUTCOME

Roman sources on the immediate results: Velleius 2.119–20; Cassius Dio 56.22; Tacitus, *Annals* 1.51, 60–62, 65; 2.10, 18, 88. On Augustus's reaction, see sources cited for chapter 4. Subsequent Roman campaigns across the Rhine: see sources cited for chapter 7. Small forts beyond the Lippe: H. Polenz, "Römer und Germanen im Raum zwischen Rhein und Weser in den ersten vier nachchristlichen Jahrhunderten," in H. G. Horn et al., eds., *Fundort Nordrhein-Westfalen* (Mainz, 2000), pp. 129–38. Waldgirmes: A. Becker and G. Rasbach, "Der spätaugusteische Stützpunkt Lahnau-Waldgirmes," *Germania* 76 (1998): 673–92. Dorlar: S. von Schnurbein and H.-J. Köhler, "Dorlar: Ein augusteisches Römerlager im Lahntal," *Germania* 72 (1994): 193–203. Roman decision to give up idea of conquering east of the lower Rhine: D. Timpe, "Der römische Verzicht auf die Okkupation Germaniens," *Chiron* 1 (1971): 267–84, and B. R. van Wickevoort Crommelin, "*Quintili Vare, legiones redde!*: Die politische und ideologische Verarbeitung einer traumatischen Niederlage," in G. Franzius, ed., *Aspekte römisch-germanischer Beziehungen in der frühen Kaiserzeit* (Espelkamp, 1995), pp. 1–43, and J. Ober, "Tiberius and the Political Testament of Augustus," *Historia* 31 (1982): 306–28.

On well-outfitted burials in the German regions in the first century A.D., see R. Busch, *Rom an der Niederelbe* (Neumünster, 1995). Feddersen Wierde: P. Schmid, "Feddersen Wierde," *Reallexikon*, vol. 8 (1994), pp. 249–66. Flögeln: W. H. Zimmermann, "Flögeln," *Reallexikon*, vol. 9 (1995), pp. 206–16. Daseburg: K. Günther, *Siedlung und Werkstätten von Feinschmieden der älteren römischen Kaiserzeit bei Warburg-Daseburg* (Münster, 1990).

12: THE MEANING OF THE BATTLE

On the later development of the Rhineland as political and cultural frontier, see H. G. Horn, ed., *Die Römer in Nordrhein-Westfalen* (Stuttgart, 1987), H. Wolfram, *The Roman Empire and Its Germanic Peoples* (Berkeley, 1997), and R. W. Southern, *The Making of the Middle Ages* (New Haven, 1959). T. O'Brien quotation: "How to Tell a True War Story," in *The Things They Carried* (New York, 1989), p. 78. Purposes of historical writing by Romans of Augustus's time: D. Timpe, "*Memoria* und Geschichtsschreibung bei den Römern," in H.-J. Gehrke and A. Möller, eds., *Vergangenheit und Lebenswelt* (Tübingen, 1996), pp. 277–99. New discoveries in Lippe valley: W. Ebel-Zepezauer and J.-S. Kühlborn, "Römer und Germanen," *Archäologie in Deutschland* 17, no. 2 (2001): 47.

Appendixes

How an Archaeological Site Is Formed
Michael B. Schiffer's *Behavioral Archeology* (New York, 1976) is a detailed study of what are known as site formation processes. For a briefer introduction to the topic, see C. Renfrew and P. Bahn, *Archaeology*, 3rd ed. (New York, 2000).

Roman Weapons Recovered at Kalkriese
An excellent overview of the finds is G. Franzius, "Die römischen Funde aus Kalkriese," in Schlüter, *Kalkriese*, pp. 107–97. On the silver trim from a scabbard, probably belonging to a Roman officer, see G. Franzius, "Beschläge einer Galdiusscheide und Teile eines *cingulum* aus Kalkriese, Ldr. Osnabrück," *Germania* 77 (1999): 567–608. The magazine *Varus-Kurier* has many good articles about the weapons found.

Frequently Cited Sources and Useful Reference Works

The Cambridge Ancient History. Vol. 10, *The Augustan Age.* Edited by S. A. Cook, F. E. Adcock, and M. P. Charlesworth. Cambridge, 1934. (Abbreviated *CAH* above)

The Cambridge Ancient History. 2nd ed. Vol. 10, *The Augustan Empire, 43 B.C.–A.D. 69.* Edited by A. K. Bowman, E. Champlin, and A. Lintott. Cambridge, 1996. (*CAH 2*)

Fansa, M., ed. *Varusschlacht und Germanenmythos.* Oldenburg, 1994.

Hornblower, S., and A. Spawforth, eds. *The Oxford Classical Dictionary.* 3rd ed. New York, 1996.

Paulys Realencyclopädie der classischen Altertumswissenschaft. Edited by G. Wissowa. Stuttgart, 1893–1972. (Pauly-Wissowa)

Reallexikon der germanischen Altertumskunde. Göttingen, 1973–2001.

Schlüter, W., ed. *Kalkriese: Römer im Osnabrücker Land.* Bramsche, 1993.

Schlüter, W., and R. Wiegels, eds. *Rom, Germanien und die Ausgrabungen von Kalkriese.* Osnabrück, 1999.

Wiegels, R., and W. Woesler, eds. *Arminius und die Varusschlacht.* Paderborn, 1995.

LATIN AND GREEK AUTHORS PUBLISHED IN THE LOEB CLASSICAL LIBRARY
(Cambridge, Mass., Harvard University Press)

The Loeb Classical Library® is a registered trademark of the President and Fellows of Harvard College.

Caesar. *The Gallic War.* Translated by H. J. Edwards (1963).

Cassius Dio. *Dio's Roman History.* Translated by E. Cary. Vols. 6 (1917) and 7 (1924).

Celsus. *De Medicina.* Translated by W. G. Spencer (1935).

Florus (Lucius Annaeus Florus). *Epitome of Roman History.* Translated by E. S. Forster (1929).

Livy. Vol. 3. Translated by B. O. Foster (1967).

Manilius. *Astronomica* 1. Translated by G. P. Goold (1977).

Ovid. *Tristia. Ex Ponto.* Translated by A. L. Wheeler (1924).

Strabo. *The Geography of Strabo.* Vol. 3. Translated by H. L. Jones (1924).

Tacitus. *The Annals.* Translated by J. Jackson. In Tacitus, vols. 3 (1931) and 4 (1970).

———— *Germania.* Translated by M. Hutton. In Tacitus, vol. 1 (1970).

Velleius Paterculus. *Compendium of Roman History.* Translated by F. W. Shipley (1924).

ACKNOWLEDGMENTS

Several units of the University of Minnesota supported the research upon which this book is based. They include the College of Liberal Arts, the Graduate School, and the McKnight Faculty Summer Fellowship and McKnight International Travel Awards programs. I thank those units for their assistance. Many people provided good advice, information, and publications that aided me in writing this book. Jack Repcheck, my editor at W. W. Norton, helped me formulate the original idea for the book, and his many valuable suggestions about a series of drafts helped turn what had begun as sometimes dense and detailed academic prose into what I hope is now a smooth and readable text. Oliver Nicholson of the University of Minnesota shared his vast knowledge of Roman history and offered much valuable advice on both major and minor issues. Stephen L. Dyson of the University of New York at Buffalo answered a number of questions about Rome and provided many valuable references. Martha Tappen of the University of Minnesota gave me good advice about scavenging animals and about bone preservation. Susanne Wilbers-Rost, Bramsche-Kalkriese, guided me around the battle site and museum in 1998 and shared her extensive knowledge about the results of the ongoing excavations. Wolfgang Schlüter, Osnabrück, sent me important publications about his archaeological investigations at Kalkriese. Other colleagues who sent publications that were valuable for the preparation of this book include Lotte Hedeager, Oslo; Steen Hvass, Copenhagen; Nico Roymans, Amsterdam; Siegmar von Schnurbein, Frankfurt; Willem Willems, Amersfoort; and Werner Zanier, Munich. Glenn Storey of the University of Iowa directed me to sources about Rome's population. My wife, Joan, and my sons, Chris and Nick, accompanied me on many research trips to sites mentioned in this book and to what may have seemed to them endless museum collections. I thank them for their patience and their good cheer.

ILLUSTRATION CREDITS

For supplying photographs, and for providing permission to reproduce published illustrations in this book, the author and publisher thank the following: Princeton University Library (frontispiece); Niedersächsische Staats- und Universitätsbibliothek, Göttingen (1); Cornell University Library, Division of Rare and Manuscript Collections (2); Susanne Wilbers-Rost, Museum und Park Kalkriese, photographs copyright Christian Grovermann for Varusschlacht im Osnabrücker Land GmbH-Museum und Park Kalkriese (4, 5, 6, 7, 8, 9, 10, 20, 28, 29); photograph copyright Grabungsteam in Kalkriese, Varusschlacht im Osnabrückner Land GmbH-Museum und Park Kalkriese (11); Metropolitan Museum of Art, New York (12); Kunsthistorisches Museum, Vienna (13); Rheinisches Landesmuseum, Bonn (14); Siegmar von Schnurbein and Römisch-Germanische Kommission, Frankfurt, from S. von Schnurbein, "Untersuchugen zur Geschichte der römishen Militärlager an der Lippe," *Bericht der Römisch-Germanischen Kommission* 62, 1981, p. 34, fig. 11, p. 46, fig. 12 (15, 16); Werner Zanier and Kommission zur vergleichenden Archäologie römischer Alpen- und Donauländer der Bayerischen Akademie der Wissenschaften, Munich (17); Flemming Bau, Aarhus (18); Michael Merkel and Helms-Museum, Hamburger Museum für Archäologie und die Geschichte Harburgs, Hamburg (19); copyright Réunion des Musées Nationaux/Art Resource, New York (the cup is in the Louvre, Paris) (21); C. Engelhardt, *Nydam Mosefund,* Copenhagen 1865, pl. 6, 3.4, 7. 15 and *Vimose Mosefundet* Copenhagen 1869, pl. 7, 26. 27 (22); Engelhardt, *Thorsbjerg Mosefund* Copenhagen 1863, p. 8, 1. 6. 11a, *Nydam Mosefund,* pl. 10, 5. 9. 10. 12. 19, *Vimos Mosfundet,* pl. 4, 2 (23); *Thorsbjerg Mosefund,* pl. 1, 1 (24); *Thorsbjerg Mosefund,* p 2, 1 (25); *Thorsbjerg Mosefund,* pl. 3, 1 (26); Bernhard Overbeck and Staatlic Münzsammlung, Munich (27); copyright Niedersächsisches Institut für h torische Küstenforschung, Wilhelmshaven, and Akademie-Verlag, Berlin (3

Map 2 is based in part on information from the map in W. Schlüter, "Archäologische Zeugnisse zur Varusschlacht," *Germania* 70, 1992, p. 310 fig 1. Map 9 is based on information from maps in S. Wilbers-Rost, "Geschichte und Ergebnisse der Ausgrabungen in Kalkriese," in Schlüter, *Kalkriese,* pp. 53–72 and W. Schlüter, "Zum stand der archäologischen Erforschung der Kalkrieser-Niewedder Senke," in Schlüter and Wiegels, *Rom,* pp. 13–60.

INDEX